TRUTH ABOUT HEALTH EXPOSED

TRUTH ABOUT
Health
EXPOSED

FE ADENIJI

Publication managed by

Matador
9 Priory Business Park,
Wistow Road, Kibworth Beauchamp,
Leicestershire. LE8 0RX
Tel: (+44) 116 279 2299
Fax: (+44) 116 279 2277
Email: books@troubador.co.uk
Web: www.troubador.co.uk/matador

Contact: info@truthabouthealthexposed.com
Website: www.truthabouthealthexposed.com

ISBN 978 0995586 307

British Library Cataloguing in Publication Data.
A catalogue record for this book is available from the British Library.

Typeset in 11pt Gill Sans Light by Troubador Publishing Ltd, Leicester, UK
Matador is an imprint of Troubador Publishing Ltd

TABLE OF CONTENTS

INTRODUCTION

Have you ever struggled to improve any aspect of your health or do you know someone who has?

The vast majority of us struggle when it comes to improving our health. This is in spite of us being aware of actions that can prevent long-term illnesses.

I believe this is partly because we are not making effective use of all the tools in our repertoire. For example, like many interventions, medicines aren't always used safely and effectively. Their misuse equates to millions being lost from the health economy. This highlights the need for supportive measures or interventions to ensure we use the tools at our disposal effectively. This book represents such an intervention. It is geared towards reducing the need for medicines used to treat long-term illnesses, whilst inspiring, enabling and empowering improvements to health through changing mindsets and approaches.

Almost two years ago, I was inspired to write a book about health after complaining to a pastor about some of the challenges I encounter in practice, with some patients refusing to adhere to advice until faced with death. Originally intentioned to be an 'idiot's guide to health,' the journey I subsequently embarked on led me to write a full-fledged book on health. Although I intended to educate and inspire others, I myself was educated and inspired by those I hoped to reach. This was in part because of what I learnt from interviewing a vast range of people. This included small and big businesses as well as experts and members of the public.

The interview process started with my desire to meet people where they were in their health journey in order to inspire and enable them to make health improvements. This gave me a powerful insight as I realized the challenge isn't necessarily the lack of knowledge, rather it is the lack of its proper application. I concluded that there needs to be more focus on addressing the barriers and hindrances to health improvement actions. For example, culture and beliefs are vital but often forgotten influences on health behaviours and people's compliance with health advice. I've addressed these in the chapters on 'Social Wellbeing' and 'Health through Faith'. Other important but largely ignored areas in preventing ill health include 'Hygiene' and 'Vaccination'. These are key infection prevention measures that, in the face of the ongoing global challenge of antimicrobial resistance, represent the best antidotes to infections. Another key topical area is cancer. Sadly, the main focus of research and media attention is treatment not prevention which was the focus here. Key to the chapter on 'Cutting Cancer Risks' was an interview I conducted with an internationally renowned Canadian cancer research scientist.

Vulnerability to long-term illnesses has increased because we work and live longer, whilst being exposed to various environmental insults. Unfortunately, most health systems are struggling to deal with this. This led me to write the chapter on 'Rising above Struggling Health Systems,' which addresses current NHS challenges and how they may be tackled from a societal and individual standpoint. An international policy expert and an executive of the Association of Medical Insurers and Intermediaries (AMII) were key contributors here.

Despite current health challenges, remember many long-term illnesses are preventable, but the onus is on you to put what you know into practice. This is why I wrote the final chapter on 'Game Changing Health Principles' to share with you principles that I believe will inspire, support and guide you in your health improvement journey.

To get the best out of this book, I would suggest for each chapter you jot down notes on what you intend to change in your life to improve your health. You may also find it helpful to use some of the tools on the website www. truthabouthealthexposed.com to help you create a plan that is unique to you.

ACKNOWLEDGEMENTS

As with most projects, there are many people without whom this book would not have been possible and although I certainly feel qualified to write a book of this nature, I would be doing a great disservice to those dedicated personnel that continue to acquire knowledge in their respective fields to claim expertise in some of the key areas I have addressed in this book. Hence, I am extremely grateful to the following people who gave their unreserved advice, help and support along the way. As well as making vital contributions, their support and engagement was a vote of confidence which kept me focused and spurred me on during the down times.

Dr John Amaechi, OBE, Ex NBA Player, High Performance Coach and Psychologist

Valerie Provan, Lead Mental Health Consultant Nurse, Cumbria Partnership NHS Foundation Trust

Dr Ewan Hunter, Consultant in HIV & Infectious Diseases, Newcastle Upon Tynes NHS Trust and Honorary Lecturer at the London School of Hygiene and Tropical Medicine

Dr Fred Martineau, Clinical Research Fellow in Health Services at the London School of Hygiene and Tropical Medicine

Leroy J Lowe, PhD, President and Co-founder of Getting to Know Cancer (NGO)

Michelle Watson, Founder of Breakfree Consultancy

I would also like to thank the Lead Pastor (**Peter Oyebola**) of the International Christian Celebration Centre, who inspired me to write a book about health, to reach out to more people. Similarly, I would like to express my gratitude to all those that partook in the interview process or offered their opinion during the process. I cannot put a price on their contributions. Last but not the least I would like to thank my dear sister for her honest criticisms and unwavering support throughout the project.

*Whilst acknowledging the support and contributions of the individuals named above, the opinions expressed in the book do not necessarily represent their viewpoint, and the author takes full responsibility for the book's content.

PART 1

THE BASICS

1

THE TRUTH ABOUT HEALTH

Have you ever wondered what it really means to be healthy? Do you consider yourself healthy? What is your yardstick for being healthy?

The health industry thrives and makes millions by telling you what you need to do or eat in order to be healthy, whilst often presenting health as a picture of 'perfect looks and physical fitness.' As a result, many of us find ourselves undergoing a constant battle to be healthy and look our best, which has led to an unhealthy focus on our physical health. This in turn leads to us spending billions on the latest health fad, supplement, diet or fitness regime, sometimes getting highly frustrated in the process as we fail to achieve 'perfect health.' This drive is what fuels the multibillion dollar health industry and ensures the pharmaceutical industry enjoys one of the highest profit margins of all business sectors. Similarly, millions are generated by health and fitness clubs and by companies producing and selling health-related products. We are living in the most scientifically advanced and knowledgeable era in history, yet weight gain, diabetes and hypertension continue to pose significant challenges to health systems worldwide. Even with our ever growing expenditures, individually and collectively or through our health systems on medications, fitness and other health products or services.

As a pharmacist, I have seen many patients having to commit to taking various medicines for long-term diseases such as hypertension, diabetes, HIV; the list goes on. In many cases the need to take such medications could have been or can be avoided by simply making a choice to live healthier. On the other hand, living healthier after a diagnosis means that the impact of a disease can be minimized or, in some cases, reversed. You see, either way, a commitment choice has to be made at some point. The question is what will it be to?

A recent survey by the UK Health and Social Care Information Centre (HSCIC, 2013) showed that almost 50% of us take prescription medications. Notably, some of the most common drugs prescribed are those for preventable conditions such as depression, high cholesterol and high blood pressure. There are many reasons for this, which in some ways is a sad reflection of the times we live in. For instance, eager to sell its products, the pharmaceutical industry continuously finds new uses for its drugs. Medication needs to be taken for these companies to stay in business; hence they often lobby governments to include these uses in various policies. In addition, our lifestyles have changed so much in the last couple of decades, and we live in an age where almost anything can be done by pressing a button. Children rarely go outside to play because of computer games. Busy lifestyles mean we get in a car for short journeys when in years gone by we would walk most places and parents would encourage their children to walk to school as opposed to driving them. Similarly, we have dish washers, washing machines, ready-made food, the list goes on… Basically, as a society, we've become victims of our own development and ingenuity by creating a 'convenient' way of life that enables us work 24 hours a day, with the ironic hope of creating a better world for ourselves; even if we don't live long enough to enjoy it!

This book, unlike many other health products and health books, isn't about giving you a long list of dos and don'ts (although there will be tips and advice along the way); rather, the emphasis will be on what true health and wellbeing is all about. The reason for this is that there is a minefield of information out there telling you what to do to be healthy, which usually involves spending money on the latest health fad, diet or weight-loss product. However, there isn't a lot out there telling you what being healthy really means, and how to manage the factors influencing your health. This, I believe, will give you a solid foundation upon which you can build and create your own 'unique' healthy, affordable and sustainable lifestyle. This will also help you decipher if the latest health fad, diet or product is relevant or useful to you and your wellbeing.

2

HEALTH AND WELLBEING –
HAVE YOU GOT IT RIGHT?

What is your honest perception of health? If your answer is the absence of disease and physical health then you are definitely not alone. In my personal experience of talking and engaging with people in health-related matters, this is the widespread perception of good health. My hope is that your perception will change by the time you finish reading this book.

Many people perceive health this way, and it is this perception that the health industry and sales of pharmaceuticals, fitness and other health-related products is built on. It is also as a direct result of the 'celebrity culture' we live in, where beauty and good looks are associated with health. Hence, plastic surgery and procedures such as breast enlargements are becoming the norm as we seek to keep up with the latest celebrity fad to the detriment of our wellbeing and ultimately our health as a whole. Please don't get me wrong; the absence of disease and physical health are important elements, but they don't do justice to the word 'health,' and they don't tell the whole story. This book seeks to explain health in its entirety, with the aim of inspiring, empowering and enabling you to improve and maintain your health in a wholesome way by working on all its elements. The methods you employ will be unique to you, and you will find that one size doesn't fit all. Some of you may need to improve one element, others two and still others all the elements. It may therefore help to formulate an action plan, which will be discussed in the later chapters.

So, let's start off by breaking down the concept of health!

Health in itself can be very broadly described, and you will probably find several definitions floating around; however, for the purpose of this book I will utilize the World Health Organization's (WHO), version which defines health as 'a state of **complete** physical, mental and social wellbeing and not merely the absence of disease or infirmity.'

Are you still with me? A simpler way of looking at health, and the key point to remember, is that the ultimate purpose of being healthy is to function efficiently and productively. In other words, if you aren't healthy you are unlikely to be functioning at maximal capacity.

Wellbeing itself goes hand in hand with health in that it helps to illustrate the fact that being healthy is also about feeling good about yourself, whilst functioning at full capacity.

In years gone by, good health meant the absence of disease, and within the medical field this was the goal. The focus was on treating disease and not necessarily about making you feel good. By and large this is still common practice today as there just isn't enough time to explore your wellbeing on a day-to-day basis. In situations where you are extremely anxious or depressed, it is likely you'll get given a pill (remember we live in a 'convenience era') or referred to a psychiatrist who may also ask you to try a pill. However, increasingly, researchers and governments are recognizing the importance of wellbeing and its link with health. For instance, it can increase your lifespan, improve recovery from illnesses and encourage positive behaviours. In addition, if you feel good it is likely those around you will too, especially from a mental and social wellbeing perspective.

There's more good news here because these effects don't just apply if you are young and healthy but also if you are elderly or have conditions such as depression, cancer, heart disease and anxiety. Furthermore, the popular saying 'there's power in positive thinking' holds true with regards wellbeing. Positive emotions are associated with greater resistance to a range of illnesses; from the common cold to a better functioning immune system.

Although WHO's definition of health will be used as a referral point, it is worth noting that the word 'complete' implies a rarely achieved ideal in reality. This often leads to an unhealthy focus on achieving perfect health and wellbeing, which in itself can lead to further problems. Hence, for the purpose of this book, and the fact that we live in the real world, we will remove the word complete and focus on the different elements in the definition. After all, it is impossible to maximize and be truly healthy if you choose to focus on just one aspect of wellbeing, for example, the purely physical.

Now, I would be lying to you if I said there are no challenges involved, but the good news is that these can all be overcome if you take a simple and balanced approach to being healthy! So whilst we explore the true meaning of health we will also discuss the challenges involved with each element, along with tips and recommendations on how to take a simple and balanced approach to produce and maintain a healthier you! So, are you still with me and are you ready to learn and let the *"Truth about Health exposed"* inspire, enable and empower you to become the healthiest you've ever been at minimal cost? Yes? Then let's proceed!

3

PHYSICAL WELLBEING (I)
'YOU ARE WHAT YOU EAT'

This is probably the most popular component because it is what many associate with health. Part of the reason for this is that it is the most visible element; you can see it and it is largely based on physical 'things' that can be measured, for example, blood pressure, weight and height .

Some of you reading this may think or have been conditioned to believe, as a result of media influence, that physical fitness and food alone drive physical wellbeing or health. That's true and those are vital aspects that we will discuss in this chapter, but they don't tell the whole story.

Whereas being active and eating healthy are vital to physical health, one aspect that is often forgotten is rest! Adequate rest and relaxation is essential for physical health. Now, I'm a stickler for abbreviations because that's how I got through pharmacy school, so the abbreviation I think will help you focus when thinking about physical wellbeing is as follows:

Look at it as if you are driving a 'CAR' towards your physical wellbeing. Now let us take a look at each element individually.

CONSUMPTION

In other words your intake because it is largely about what you eat and drink. The popular saying 'you are what you eat' forms the essence of this section and the importance of a healthy diet. Often times we try to take short cuts and fail to eat a healthy diet for reasons such as living a busy life or trying to keep up with the latest health fad (which may include a diet lacking essential nutrients) or even a simple lack of awareness of foods that should be eaten in small quantities or avoided altogether. Some of us also feel we can get away with substituting proper foods with various supplements.

Unfortunately, the realization and appreciation of the importance of eating the right food tends to hit many as they get older. This is often at a point when much of the damage has been done. For instance, your blood vessels may already be clogged with cholesterol and fat that has accumulated after years of having an unhealthy diet (see Figure 1), which in turn leads to various heart and circulatory problems. Similarly, diabetes and other illnesses often arise because of the cumulative effect of years of unhealthy living.

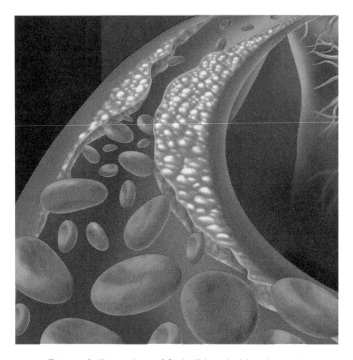

Figure 1. Illustration of fat build-up in blood vessels.
Image from iStock.

With ageing, our metabolic rate naturally starts to slow down. In addition, many of us tend to be less active as we get older, resulting in a greater struggle with weight gain. To make matters even more challenging, we find that the weight comes on easy but is difficult to lose. This is more so when we eat the wrong food. On the flip side, some of us become so obsessed with our weight that we starve ourselves and exercise excessively to maintain a low and unhealthy weight. It goes without saying that neither of these extremes are a healthy option. Rather, the key to maintaining a healthy weight is your diet because a healthy diet equals a healthy weight, and this translates to good health, especially in conjunction with the 'A' and 'R' elements, which we'll discuss later.

Now, I know we all like stats so I thought I'd show you just how much of a problem this is globally (oh yes, you are definitely not alone in the struggle to eat healthy).

According to WHO, as recent as 2014 there were almost two billion overweight people across the world, and, contrary to popular belief, malnourishment is widespread in both developed and developiong countries.[1] Surprisingly, the causes are similar, in that poverty and illiteracy are strongly linked to unhealthy diets. One driver that often gets forgotten is marketing by the food industry. The food industry, including fast-food companies, spends billions every year on advertising to young people. An American study back in 2009 by obesity action coalition claimed at least 51% of food marketing was for products such as sugary drinks, cereals, sweets, salty snacks and fast food.[2] Although these figures can't be directly extrapolated to the UK because of societal and cultural differences, they do highlight the intensity of the marketing strategies employed by producers of 'junk food.' They often employ a variety of creative strategies ranging from TV adverts to celebrity endorsements and social media adverts, for example coca cola had 84 million likes on Facebook back in 2014; up by 174% from 2011![2] They continuously target young people in particular as does the tobacco industry, they know that if they 'get them young they'll keep them.' By increasing brand awareness amongst young people, they are likely to ensure that they will stick with their brands through adulthood because many of us are creatures of habit. These companies have the money to spend both on advertising and lobbying the government; sometimes influencing the introduction of key policies that may affect use of their products. They have little, if any, competition, so it is largely down to you as an individual to be aware of what you should be eating and feeding your children.

Unfortunately, current statistics indicate the vast majority of us are struggling in this area as 65% of men and 58% of women are considered overweight or obese according to Public Health England (PHE). However, all is not lost as the good news is that eating healthy and maintaining a healthy weight-

1. Doesn't have to be complicated with numerous numbers, and
2. Doesn't have to involve large amounts of money.

All that is required is a choice to structure your food intake around what you are about to learn. Importantly, the principles stated here will also help you if you've ever had issues with keeping weight off.

A HEALTHY 'INTAKE'

A healthy intake is about eating a healthy diet, that is to say a diet that has the right amount of energy and the various nutrients required to enable your body to function efficiently and effectively, ideally to maximal capacity. Straight away you can see that if you eat healthy then you automatically should be able to maintain a healthy weight. This is the weight at which your body is able to function properly and at full capacity. To illustrate this further, I will refer to a time when, as a junior pharmacist, I worked on a bariatric ward; a ward where overweight and obese patients were admitted to before and after surgical procedures to reduce their weight and ensure they remain a 'healthy size.' Many of these patients were on several medications before the procedure because they suffered from physical conditions such as asthma and diabetes. I found it amazing that most of their medicines could be stopped after surgery. This was because their physical health automatically improved with weight reduction, such that their body was able to function better. In addition, because they had less weight on them it was easier for them to live healthier. Most overweight people, as many of them have testified, feel much better when they are a healthy weight. In fact, like me, you might have experienced this yourself when your weight has fluctuated. I've often found that I feel lighter and much more effective after losing weight I may have gained over, say Christmas.

There is an extensive amount of information out there about food and eating or drinking healthy. Personally, I think it is an overload of information which can be quite confusing, so I tend to take a simple approach to my diet, and that's what I'll do here; keep things simple because many of us gain weight by unknowingly eating diets rich in saturated and trans fats, which, together with excess salt and sugar, are a recipe or 'diet' for disaster.

There are several schools of thought about what a healthy diet entails, but for the sake of simplicity, and our increasingly diverse population, I will aim to be as comprehensive and inclusive as possible.[5, 6]

Generally speaking, the bulk of your diet should be based on cereals such as rice, corn, wheat, pasta, spaghetti, oats, garri (eba), millet, and fruit and vegetables along with pulses such as chick peas and beans. To break the proportions down further:

1. **Carbohydrates:** The bulk of your diet (i.e. around half of your total energy intake) should be from this group, with added sugars (more detail below) accounting for less than 10%.

   Tip: *Choose wholegrain over white or refined starches to be fuller for longer*

2. **Protein:** This should account for about a sixth of your diet (15%). Ensure a sizeable proportion of these are from plant sources such as beans, unsalted nuts and lentils. **Tip:** *Lean and unprocessed meat is best.*

3. **Fat:** Less than 30% of your diet. Try to avoid 'bad' fats (i.e. saturated and trans) found in food like fatty meat, palm oil, butter, ghee, cheese, processed or fried foods and flour-based snacks. Rather, try and ensure the bulk of your fat intake is from foods such as avocado, sunflower/olive oil and oily fish (i.e. mono- and poly-unsaturated 'good' fats).
    Tip: *Reduce your fat intake by limiting intake of processed foods and snacks.*

4. **Free sugars:** Less than 10% of your diet (~12 level teaspoons). These include sugars refined by humans that are added to food or drinks during manufacture or cooking. They are also present in honey, syrups and fruit juices.

5. **Salt:** No more than 5 grams per day (~ 1 teaspoon). Be aware, most processed foods contain significant amounts of salt. Most of us consume between 9 and 12 grams per day, about double the recommended amount.

6. **Fruit and Vegetables:** Aim to eat at least 5 portions, or 400 grams per day.

The table on the following page illustrates the proportions further, with some examples. Feel free to use it as a reference when fine tuning your diet.

Table 1.

Nutrient	Proportion of daily diet (in simple terms)	Examples	Comments
Carbohydrates	Half	Rice, corn, cassava, wheat, yam, oats	
Protein	About a sixth	Beans, lentils, meat, unsalted nuts	Better to have more from plant-based sources
		Fish Oily: Salmon, mackerel, fresh tuna, Others: Cod, prawns	Aim for 2 portions per week (including one oily fish)
Fat	Up to a third	**'Bad' fat:** Cheese, palm oil, processed food, flour-based snacks	Ensure bulk is 'good' fat
		'Good' fat: Sunflower/olive oil, avocado, oily fish	
'Free' Sugars – added to food/ drinks	Up to 10% (~12 level teaspoons)	Present in honey, sweets, fruit juices and fruit juice concentrates	The less the better
Salt	Up to 5 grams (1 teaspoon)		Watch out for snacks and processed food

Fruit and Vegetables	At least 5 portions	Apples, spinach, kiwi	A single fruit or 3 heaped tablespoons of vegetables is equivalent to a portion
Fluids	6 to 8 glasses or cups	Water, fruit juices, tea, coffee	≤150mls fruit juice/ smoothies Less is better for high fat, sugar- or salt- containing drinks

It is also important to be aware of so-called healthy snacks such as packaged popcorn as they often contain 'bad' fats to make them more palatable.

As far as sugars go, try and stick to natural sweeteners such as honey, they are less processed and retain some nutrients such as trace elements and vitamins, compared to white sugar, which has hardly any nutritional value. In addition, despite being similar in calorie content, you are likely to need less honey than sugar for the same sweetness effect because of its density, although this is not a license to substitute sugar with honey regularly. Over time it may help reduce your calorie and free sugar intake. Artificial sweeteners are also reasonable alternatives as they have minimal caloric value, with limited effect on blood sugar or links with dental decay. They are also economical.

Use the table on the previous page to monitor your food intake and make adjustments if need be. For instance, if you are trying to lose weight, it may be that you want to keep fat and sugar content to a minimum, whilst increasing your protein content and keeping your carbohydrates to a minimum.

There are a number of other actions you can take to ensure you take the healthiest of diets, including avoiding fried and processed foods that are rich in bad fats, free sugars, and salt. Where possible, try to eat and cook using fresh produce.

Note, the above diet is geared towards the standard adult, and it will differ slightly for children and those with particular medical conditions including pregnancy. Nonetheless, the general principles will remain the same, so you can still use it as a guide. However in such scenarios, you may also want to consider seeking advice from a health professional.

This diet should help you maintain a healthy weight, especially alongside regular physical activity (which we'll discuss later). The diet should add up to 2000 Kcal for a woman and 2500 Kcal for a man.[7] However, should you be aiming to lose weight, you may want to reduce your caloric intake. For example, you could aim to have a total of 1400 Kcal split throughout the day. Having said this, please don't get obsessed with numbers. Instead, consider reducing your portion size, and the amount of processed food and snacks you eat. There are a lot of conflicting views pertaining to the proportion and types of carbohydrates or fats you should be taking from a health and weight-loss perspective. My advice is that, although one size doesn't fit all, you shouldn't get too lost in the science or bogged down with technicalities.

Rather, aim to keep things simple and get the basics right for you. By doing this and following the guidelines discussed here, whilst using the table and picture below as guides, you should make considerable progress.

Weight-loss tip: *Swap your meals so that your bulk intake is for breakfast, followed by lunch and a very light meal for dinner e.g. 700 Kcal for breakfast, with 500 and 200 Kcal for lunch and dinner respectively.*[9]

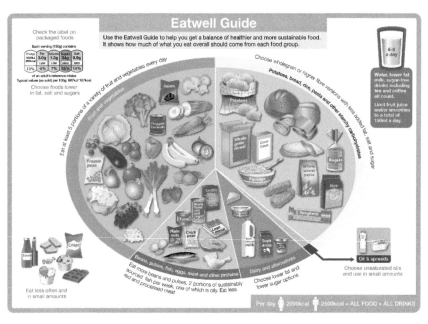

Source: Public Health England in association with the Welsh Government, Food Standards Scotland and the Food Standard Agency in Northern Ireland

© Crown copyright 2016

Figure 2. *From Public Health England's Eat well guide updated 24th August 2016*

As I bring this section to a close, I'd like to highlight two important cautions:

1. Diet fads! They often lack the necessary nutrients required to be healthy. For instance, they may be excessively high in protein and low in carbohydrate, which can increase nausea, fatigue, blood pressure, and the risk of cancer, etc.
2. Aim to lose no more than 0.5 to 1 kg per week until you reach your 'ideal' weight.

Please note, I haven't included much about vitamins and minerals here because I discuss them later in the book. However, bear in mind that if you eat a balanced diet it is inevitable that you get an adequate amount of required nutrients. Personally, I am not a massive fan of supplements in the absence of specific circumstances such as pregnancy, malnutrition, or poor dietary intake as I believe every effort should go towards having a balanced diet rather than taking a pill.

REFERENCES:

1. World Health Organisation (WHO). Obesity and Overweight Factsheet. Updated June 2016.
2. Dolce M (MA). UConn Rudd Centre for Food Policy and Obesity. Obesity Action Coalition. Food Marketing to Children: A Wolf in Sheep's Clothing? Summer 2015; 10:4.
3. Ossei- Assiby G, Dick S, MacDiarmid J Et al. British Medical journal, December 2012. Public Health- The influence of

the food environment on overweight and obesity in young children: a systematic review. (BMJ Open 2012; e001538 doi: 10-11 36/bmjopen-2012-001538).

4. Health and Social Care Information Centre, England. Statistics on Obesity, Physical Activity and Diet. Published April 2016.

5. World Health Organisation (WHO). Healthy Diet Fact Sheet No 394. Updated September 2015.

6. Public Health England. Eat Well Guide. Updated 24 August 2016.

7. National Institute for Health and Care Excellence (NICE). Clinical Guidance CG189, Published November 2014. Obesity: Identification, Assessment and Management.

8. Public Health Collaboration. Healthy Eating Guidelines and Weight Loss Advice for the United Kingdom, 2016.

9. Jakubowicz D, Barnea M, Wainstein J Et al. Obesity, March 2013. High caloric intake at breakfast vs dinner differentially influences weight loss of overweight and obese women. Obesity 2013; 21(12): 2504- 2512.

4

PHYSICAL WELLBEING (II)
'STAY ACTIVE AND RECHARGE'

RELAX...

This is probably the one element of physical health that is rarely talked about. Its link with health is often overlooked. The world we live in encourages us to live life on the go. Hence, we eat on the go, work on the go, and, thanks to the likes of Apple and Microsoft, we can now holiday on the go. We just can't let go or switch off! We tend to see it as a badge of honour to function for several hours without end.

Well, I have some news for you. If you want to be truly healthy then just as you invest in healthy food, exercise routines, medical care, or treatments, you must also invest in relaxing and resting. Ironically, of all aspects of physical health, relaxing and resting are probably the most cost effective. They are free to engage in unless you have chronic sleep problems, in which case you may want to seek professional help or advice.

So, what does it mean to relax, and what does it mean to rest? The two terms are very similar, but they have subtle differences that should be considered when creating a routine for them. The Cambridge dictionary defines rest as the cessation of activity for a period of time in order to regain strength. Similarly, it explains relaxation as becoming less active and more calm and happy. In reality, the two terms go hand in hand as in both situations the goal is to be calm and less active in order to regain your strength.

Resting is so important that even God, the one that many believe created the Universe, needed to take a day off to rest, and if he did, then how much more us mere mortals? The fact is we all need adequate rest that we get through sleep, which involves total cessation of physical activities and by relaxation which involves engaging in activities that help to keep you calm. Now, you definitely don't need a book or expert to tell you how important it is for you to get some sleep, as without it you're likely to become groggy and unable to function, whereas with it you feel strengthened and re-energized. Such is the importance of sleep that the Harvard Medical School has an entire division dedicated to it and actually rates it in the same class as nutrition and regular physical activity in regards to health.[3] However, it often gets overlooked by the health industry (probably because there's not as much money to be made by telling people to sleep).

Be honest. How often have you tried improving your diet or exercise routine? Now, how often have you tried improving your sleep or rest pattern? If you're anything like me a few years back then the answer to the latter question is probably that you've never really thought about it.

Let me use myself to illustrate this point. Some time ago I changed jobs, and I was averaging four to five hours sleep per night. Before I knew it I was getting breakouts. I spent a lot of time playing with my diet as I thought it might be something I'd eaten, when that didn't work I started changing my skin products to no effect. Then by chance someone mentioned that I must be going through a stressful period. This made me stop and think about other less obvious changes I had made. I realized that my sleep pattern had become irregular due to the change in my work environment and a considerable amount of travel. I then re-organized myself and my day to ensure my sleeping pattern was more regular and adequate. Bingo! My face cleared up. Now, this is a more obvious example of why adequate rest is important and the need for you to be conscious about changes in your life circumstances that may impact it. There are, however, other reasons it is important; both from a long- and short-term perspective.

Short-term benefits include increased alertness, efficiency and productivity in carrying out various tasks whether in school or work.[3] In addition, better focus helps avoid the consequences of serious lapses of concentration, such as car accidents. In the long term, research is starting to show a strong link between lack of sleep and chronic medical conditions such as inflammation, diabetes, and high blood pressure, etc.[3] Without being too scientific, lack of sleep is inevitably associated with increased stress and anxiety, which is linked to hypertension. This in turn can lead to other chronic conditions such as diabetes and kidney problems. Furthermore, adequate rest makes you look good! For instance, well-rested people often look younger as cell renewal is done more efficiently at night.[3] I guess I'm a prime example of that as I definitely look better without spots (at least I hope I do!).

OK, now we know sleep is important, the next question is how much do you need?

The amount of sleep required is somewhat individualistic, but evidence suggests on average six to nine hours of sleep per night is ideal, with requirements increasing with extremes of age.[1, 2, 3] Studies have also shown that those who get less than this are more likely to gain weight.[1, 2] Such is the importance of sleep in weight gain that lack of it is now being mentioned as a risk factor along with a lack of exercise and over eating. Lack of sleep increases cravings for sweet foods in order to get quick energy boosts. This can obviously contribute to weight gain, and is worsened by the fact that such an individual is likely to be too tired to burn off the extra calories through exercise.[1,2] Generally speaking, if you feel alert and refreshed on waking then you've probably had enough sleep.

So, I hope you feel encouraged to keep a check on your sleep pattern because although you may be able to function on less than the recommended number of hours a night, you may find that you function even better by adjusting your sleep pattern. In addition, don't forget when you sleep cell rejuvenation, immune system strengthening, healing and repair of vital organs occur. These all contribute to your health and wellbeing in the short and long term.[3]

Now, I know there are many that genuinely struggle to sleep because they suffer from chronic insomnia or other disorders like depression and anxiety. In such scenarios, it is worth seeking help from a sleep therapist. For less severe cases, there are a number of remedies available over the counter that can help, so consider popping into your local pharmacy for advice on which will suit you best. Please be aware that it is best to use these remedies on a short-term basis only because some of them are addictive and tolerance can develop over time such that they become ineffective; furthermore, if you need to use them long term then there may be an underlying problem that needs further investigation.

In other cases, it may be that you need to tweak your lifestyle a bit in order to get more quality rest such as avoiding caffeine (present in coffee, tea, coke, etc.), spicy food, sugar treats, nicotine or other related chemicals at least three to six hours before going to sleep. Alcohol is another substance of which to be mindful. Although a weak sedative, it often decreases the quality of sleep. Thus it's worth avoiding in the immediate hours before sleep as well as staying within recommended daily limits. Also try to decrease your fluid intake just before bedtime so you are not constantly waking up to urinate.

PHYSICAL WELLBEING (II)

Generally speaking, you may find it helpful to create a cool, quiet, and dark environment by blocking out light. For example, heavy curtains, blackout shades, etc., whilst making your room cozy and comfortable with minimal work-related items in view e.g. laptops can help. You may also find it useful to avoid 'screen-time' from back lit screens such as mobile devices and the television as the light emitted can prevent the release of melatonin which helps control your sleep cycle. In addition, some find it helpful to have a calm pre-sleep routine e.g., having a bath, watching television and relaxation exercises.

To finish off this section, I'm going to talk a little bit about relaxation. Although sleep is the ultimate form of rest, relaxation and maintaining a state of calmness is also very important to reduce tension and maintain wellbeing. It is probably just as important as sleep, but can get overlooked as, between working and sleeping; it is easy to forget to allow time to unwind. Now, different things relax different people, for me I feel most relaxed when I'm playing basketball or engaging in sport activity. That may seem strange because many may feel an activity such as reading a book or watching television is more relaxing and that may well be the case for some. However, the point is that you take time out to engage in an activity that helps to calm your mind and makes you happy at the same time.

Now, I'm a massive advocate for working hard, but I'm not an advocate for working yourself to an early grave.

Hence, whatever job, goals, or ambitions you have, endeavour to organize your schedule to allow time for adequate rest and relaxation activities.

GET ACTIVE!!!

Being active with the ultimate aim of improving physical fitness is probably the most popular aspect of physical wellbeing. It's the reason why many folks sign up to gyms in January. Fitness refers to your ability to perform physical activities and is often based on a range of factors such as endurance, strength, flexibility, speed, and power. This ability can be improved upon through engaging in various activities.

Inevitably fitness levels are individualistic as they depend on factors such as genetics, previous fitness levels, gender and age. From a health perspective, fitness is about being able to perform various activities regularly and comfortably. Note the words 'regularly' and 'comfortably' not 'strenuously' or 'excessively'! The point being that you should not allow yourself to be pressurised into being mega fit or feel the need to do excessive amounts of exercise to be healthy. The truth is that with regular bouts of activity your fitness levels will improve naturally.

'FITNESS' AND PHYSICAL WELLBEING

Being fit means you ensure the physical condition of your heart, muscles and lungs are in good shape and able to function at maximal capacity. This will translate to reductions in blood pressure and weight as well as improvements in blood sugar control and bone strength. The end result of all this is a longer and healthier lifespan. Thus there is no time like the present to commit to exercising regularly. The key word here is 'routine' as developing one will help ensure you maintain a healthy fitness level, whilst maximizing your physical wellbeing. Furthermore, being fit isn't just about preventing diseases. It is also about productivity as it helps you think better and more creatively. In fact, the great American philosopher and author Henry Thoreau claimed that his 'thoughts began to flow the moment his legs began to move' and many others testify to this. I personally find that after exercising, especially after doing something that I enjoy, I'm at my most relaxed. I'm thereafter more creative and productive in my thinking.

The benefits don't stop there as exercise can act as a detox via generation of sweat. This is especially important during cold weather when you are less likely to sweat naturally. Sweat is one of the ways your body gets rid of toxins and cleanses itself! I know, the benefits of developing an exercise routine are amazing aren't they? So start one today if you haven't already got one!

So how do you start and how much should you be doing? This can be as complicated as you let it. You don't need to sign up to a gym to be fit; as a brisk walk on a regular basis can help you maintain good physical health and wellbeing. Consider using the following as a guide regardless of what activity you do currently.[4]

1. Five 30-minute sessions per week of moderate intensity activities, e.g. cycling or brisk walking.

    OR

2. Three 20-minute sessions per week of vigorous intensity activities, e.g. jogging or aerobics.
   OR

3. Mix the above types of activities, e.g. two 30-minute brisk walks and two 20-minute jogs.

These options will help ensure you meet the minimum target of 150 minutes of exercise per week (recommended by Public Health England). Where possible, try to do a mixture of activities of mixed intensities, e.g. weight bearing (walking, running, some weight lifting) and high-impact exercises involving jumping and resistance (carrying heavy shopping, press-ups, free weights) to ensure maximal benefit from exercising.[4] There are many other exercises you could do and incorporate into your lifestyle for practicality. Why not take the stairs instead of using the escalator or the lift? Or even park further away so you are forced to walk.

You'll be surprised how such activities can add up to form a crucial part of recommended levels of activities. For instance, walking 10,000 steps per day is equivalent to walking briskly for about 75 minutes. If you were to do even half of this a couple of times a week you would easily hit the 150-minute minimum weekly target. Better still, if you did it daily it would enable you burn 400 Kcal daily, which could help you lose weight in line with the recommendation to reduce your daily calorie intake by at least 600 Kcal in order to lose weight.[6]

In addition to being active, it is crucial you recognise the need to be less sedentary. According to Public Health England many of us spend more than seven hours a day being sedentary! I know being less sedentary is sometimes hard with current working practices, but there are simple things you can do to limit this, such as watching less television, not sitting continuously at work, standing whilst commuting etc.

FAT AND WEIGHT LOSS TIPS: [4]

1. *Involuntary movements such as standing and fidgeting can contribute to increased energy expenditures of up to 350 Kcal.*
2. *Two minutes of stair climbing each day can burn enough calories to eliminate the weight an average adult gains in a year*

These recommendations apply to pretty much everyone and abstinence isn't an option. The regimen can be tailored to suit you, even if you have a disability or poor health. It is just a matter of seeking professional guidance in those scenarios.

A point worth mentioning here is that the options above are a minimum guide more appropriate to maintain health. If you are aiming to maintain your weight, especially after losing it, then the regimen needs to change slightly by increasing the duration of exercise by 15–30 minutes daily. If you are trying to lose weight, then as well as doing more exercise, reduce your food intake. Please note that as far as losing and maintaining weight goes, keep it simple by listening and being aware of what your body is telling you. Quite often you'll know when you've put on some weight, and that might be an indication to increase the duration for a bit whilst reducing your food intake, similarly there may be times when you've overdone it and need to tone things down on the exercise front, whilst increasing your food intake.

To help support you in applying the above points, I'm going to finish the chapter by giving you some advice on how to keep a check on your physical health, and make sure you're doing things right.

KNOW YOUR NUMBERS!

So now I have discussed the different components of your physical health and you're about to action some of the tips mentioned in order to attain 'perfect' physical health, how do you know you are on the right track and taking effective action?

The answer is by knowing your numbers!

There are three key numbers to know, especially if you are over 40. Fortunately, within the NHS, it is free, and a legal entitlement, to have a complete risk assessment if you are over 40. However, I would still advise you to have this done if you are under 40 as it will give you a baseline to work from. It is easily accessible and can be done by popping into your local pharmacy or GP, where the practice nurse can do it for you. Some gyms now do this as part of what's called a health 'MOT', so you can also ask for it to be done there.

So what numbers do you need to be aware of?

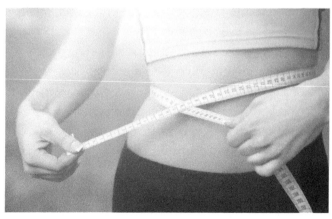

Figure 4. Measurements of BMI and waist circumference.
Images from iStock

1. BMI (Body Mass Index): This gives you an idea of whether you are of a healthy weight in proportion with your height. It does have some limitations, and if you find yours outside normal range don't panic. Consult a health care professional to help you interpret it.

2. Waist circumference or size: This is a very good indicator of fat around your abdomen, which is the worst place to accumulate fat compared to places like the bottom or hips. Fat around the waist is associated with cardiovascular disease, hypertension and diabetes. Some people actually believe this is a bigger risk factor than having a high BMI. It is therefore advised as an alternative and extra check.

3. Blood Pressure: Knowing this means you can keep it in check. NHS figures state 1 in 3 people in England have high blood pressure, but most are unaware. A significant proportion of these are people under 60 years of age, and if you're of ethnic minority origin your risks are likely to be even higher. It is often called the 'silent killer' because you need to check it to know it and control it in order to prevent more serious conditions like a stroke or heart attack occurring. The good news is that high blood pressure can be reversed, especially in the early stages; another reason to keep a check on it.

4. Cholesterol: This is a fatty substance that is important for normal body functioning such as manufacture of key hormones and processing of some vitamins. Too much of it, however, clogs your blood vessels and hinders blood flow, which increases your risk of a stroke or heart attack. It is also associated with diabetes. It is

useful to be aware of your levels, regardless of age, if you are overweight, smoke, have a heart condition or diabetes in your family.

Where possible, you may find it helpful to have these numbers checked out and discussed with a health professional. Knowing them will enable you take more control of your health and wellbeing. It will also ensure you take more informed actions as well as access relevant support to help maintain your physical wellbeing in the long term.

REFERENCES:

1. Patel SR, Malhotra A, White D, et al. American Journal of Epidemiology, Nov 2006. Association between reduced sleep and weight gain in women. Am J Epidemiol, 2006; 164(10): 947-954.
2. Patel SR and Hu FB. Obesity, Mar 2008. Short sleep duration and weight gain. Obesity, 2008; 16(3): 643- 653.
3. http://healthysleep.med.harvard.edu/. Accessed November 2016.
4. Public Health England, July 2016. Health Matters: Getting Every Adult Active Everyday
5. www.i-base.info. Updated September 2016. Accessed November 2016.
6. National Institute for Health and Care Excellence (NICE). Clinical Guidance CG189, Published November 2014. Obesity: Identification, Assessment and Management.

5

MENTAL HEALTH AND WELLBEING
'MAINTAINING POSITIVITY THROUGH STRATEGIC ACTIONS'

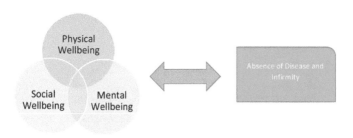

According to WHO, mental health and wellbeing is the second component of health that must be addressed to achieve a state of general wellbeing. Unfortunately, its link with health is often misunderstood and underestimated as many are quick to associate it with disorders such as schizophrenia, bipolar or depression. However, this provides a false conception of mental health and wellbeing as it is much more than that, and applies to us all.

Let us take a look at some of the definitions floating around:

Wikipedia explains it as *"a level of psychological wellbeing, or absence of a mental disorder in that it is the* '*psychological state of someone functioning at a satisfactory level of emotional and behavioural adjustment."*

Psychology looks at it from a positive psychological viewpoint in that it includes *"a person's ability to enjoy life, and create a balance between life activities and efforts to achieve psychological resilience."*

As usual, WHO gives a very comprehensive definition that includes the above definitions and more. It defines it as:

".... a state of wellbeing in which the individual realizes his or her own abilities, can cope with the normal stresses of life, work productively and fruitfully and is able to make a contribution to his or her community..."

The key phrase to remember here is "state of mind." Good mental health and wellbeing is about feeling good within one's self and having the capacity to take on the daily challenges that life throws at us, without developing a psychiatric illness or abusing recreational substances such as alcohol, cocaine or cannabis. Hence, it is important to be aware that mental wellbeing is not just about the absence of mental disorders; rather, it is also about having a 'positive' state of mind regardless of environmental pressures.

Having a full grasp of what good mental health and wellbeing entails is vital if you want to maintain a positive state of mind. For a long time, the impact and importance of mental health and wellbeing has been underestimated to the detriment of society at large. Being mentally impaired doesn't just affect you as an individual. Unlike many other physical illnesses, it has a significant impact on others in your environment and the wider society as a whole. A good example of this can be seen in the life of an addict, where their poor mental wellbeing and inability to cope with life's challenges leads them down the path of addiction. This in turn results in them carrying out various negative actions such as stealing from and hurting, in some cases abusing, those closest to them.

At a societal level, poor mental wellbeing is a major contributor to decreased productivity in the workforce, as evidenced by the fact that in 2015/16, stress accounted for 45% of all working days lost because of ill health.[1] In addition, the annual cost attributed to this issue is £5.2 billion.[1] Considering the other costs, financial and otherwise, to the sufferer and their family, it is difficult not to appreciate how important mental wellbeing is in order to ensure you are able to operate productively and to full capacity.

MENTAL AND PHYSICAL WELLBEING, THE CONNECTION

Mental wellbeing is closely related to physical wellbeing.

The two constantly interact. Many people with chronic illnesses go on to develop some type of mental health disorder. This could be caused by a range of factors, but is often closely linked to poor coping mechanisms. Similarly, those with mental health disorders are more likely to develop physical illnesses; for example, stress and anxiety can lead to hypertension, which in turn can lead to other conditions. Stress may also lead to comfort eating, which leads to weight gain and obesity, which can lead to diabetes. More serious consequences of mental health disorders such as drug and alcohol addiction can cause liver damage. A resulting accumulation of various toxins leads to a host of other clinical problems, which can lead to death in the absence of effective treatment or a transplant.

From a social perspective, poor mental wellbeing is closely related to a low self-esteem, poor coping mechanisms and difficulties in forging and developing positive relationships with others. This is what fuels various criminal activities such as addictions, rape, sexual abuse, domestic violence and gang membership, which in itself leads to increased crime and attacks. Sadly, the knock-on effect of this is not just on the victims or perpetrators who are victims in themselves, but their families and society as a whole.

With one in ten children aged 5 to 16 alleged to have a clinically diagnosed mental health disorder and one in four adults diagnosed annually, you cannot afford to put the psychological wellbeing of you and your family to the side when trying to improve and maintain your health.[7]

DEALING WITH THE 'SHAME' OF POOR MENTAL WELLBEING

The sad thing with poor mental health and wellbeing is the stigma that goes with it. Similar to conditions such as

HIV, there appears to be deep-rooted shame in confessing one's mental wellbeing or health isn't 100%. This shame and stigma applies not just to the sufferers but to close family members who are often ashamed to be related to someone with poor mental health. This creates a vicious cycle as they are unable to get the full range of support, including vital social networks needed to conquer the issue. Similarly, the shame can prevent family members from accessing the right support to help them cope and be an effective supporting mechanism.

At this point I would like to say that seeking help is one of the first steps you can take to improve your mental wellbeing or that of a close friend or relative. The worst thing you can do is try to bear the burden alone as that starts to gradually impact on your mental health, predisposing you to a mental disorder if you haven't already got one. As indicated by the statistics, mental health disorders are very common and are often reflective of a number of situations, so don't hesitate to seek help or support where needed. There is *no shame in being unaware, but there is shame in doing nothing when aware because you are scared of other people's perceptions.*

Now, it is important to mention that there are several factors outside the scope of this book that can impact mental health and wellbeing. Some of which you will have no control over as an individual. However, the good news is that you can control your own mind and perspective on things. You can do this by choosing to be optimistic and happy in the face of challenges, whilst improving your self-esteem and resilience.

To help you overcome the challenges you face and develop the characteristics you need to maintain a positive state of mind, let us take a look at some of the main factors that can affect your mental wellbeing.

FACTORS AFFECTING MENTAL WELLBEING

There is extensive information available on the varying factors that can affect your mental health and wellbeing; however, for simplicity I will base my groupings loosely on those suggested by WHO – "coping" characteristics, social and economic circumstances, and the wider environment.[2] Now let us take a look a deeper look at each one of these.

"Coping" Characteristics

This particular factor is essentially about your ability to cope with your thoughts and feelings on a daily basis. This is your capacity to deal with the day-to-day challenges life presents to us. Now, your ability to cope is closely related to your social world. This entails your ability to interact with others in a productive fashion, which may also involve participation in social activities. This is where you need to be careful with the people you surround yourself with as quite often they can influence your mental wellbeing. If you have the wrong social circle, it is likely your mental wellbeing will be affected in a negative way. Key message here: Surround yourself with positive people!

Yes, it is true your ability to cope is also affected by

factors you have minimal control over, such as your genes, exposure to toxic substances such as alcohol before you were born, drug addiction and trauma such as brain injuries. However, you can rise above these factors and improve your coping capacity by focusing on what you can control, such as your mind-set and the people around you.

Social and Economic Factors

It is a known and unfortunate fact that many people with poor mental health come from a disadvantaged background. In fact a number of studies testify to this as they have shown an increased rate of mental health disorders such as depression and anxiety among immigrant populations such as Black Africans and Asians.[3] The link between background and mental health has also been noted in Caucasian working-class populations adding further weight to the suggestion that the link is due to such populations being disadvantaged in terms of their ability to earn an income, level of education and employment status.[3, 4, 5] For immigrants, they often have the added challenge of culturally adapting to and being accepted by their host community.

Some of the solutions to this lay outside traditional health-sector boundaries and are beyond the scope of this book, but by increasing your awareness around these issues you can empower yourself and those around you to rise above the limitations of your immediate environment.

Environmental Factors

Environmental factors refer to the things in your surroundings that impact mental wellbeing. It includes government policies that enable you to access basic amenities such as water, food, good housing and education. It also encompasses events such as the global financial crises in 2008, which is thought to have led to an increase in suicide rates secondary to job losses.[6]

Another crucial factor that often gets overlooked is culture. The culture and cultural beliefs within your environment have a massive impact on your behaviour and lifestyle – both of which contribute to your mental wellbeing. For instance, a culture that encourages spirituality can help improve your coping capacity in tough times. Thus, it is important to be aware of the cultural practices and beliefs that influence your behaviours and lifestyle so you can make necessary adaptations.

Now, as I mentioned earlier, there are some of you that may have experienced or been a victim of tough circumstances with no effect on your mental health.

That's where tolerance and vulnerability comes in. We all have different thresholds for different things. For example, some people can tolerate pain to a large degree because they have a high pain threshold. Others can tolerate higher doses of drugs before being adversely affected. Some people that abuse drugs develop mental disorders such as schizophrenia, whilst others don't. The reason is that they are already vulnerable to developing these diseases. Unfortunately, we don't have a crystal ball so can't predict with certainty who is or isn't going to get these diseases. However, the good news is that we can predict vulnerability to these diseases by looking at some key driving factors for mental health disorders, which include[2]:

- Poverty
- Chronic illnesses
- Minority status
- Exposure to conflicts

Once you are predisposed to a mental health disorder driven by any of the aforementioned, there is a possibility that the disorder could be worsened by the stigma, discrimination and social exclusion associated with mental health disorders.

It is important to talk about these factors here as, essentially, when faced with these issues, a vicious cycle often occurs. Anxiety, depression, insecurity and a decrease in self-esteem can arise, amongst other things. These are somewhat normal reactions to challenging situations; however, as humans, our ability to cope differs significantly and is based on a number of other factors such as our support network and spirituality. The next section discusses ways of improving coping capacities whilst maintaining mental wellbeing.

TAKE A CHILL PILL

So now we've looked at the main driving factors, the question is how do you stop your mental health and wellbeing from becoming a victim of them?

There are numerous ways to maintain or improve your wellbeing and the approach you take should be individualistic. In other words, 'do you'! Don't worry about what other people are doing because the factors listed above affect us all differently. Below is a list of actions you may want to take to help you devise a plan to improve your mental health and wellbeing. They are applicable regardless of whether or not you have a mental disorder. Also, use the list as a guide to support a friend or relative you know that may be struggling with their mental wellbeing.

Actions to Improve Mental Health and Wellbeing

1. Change your mind-set:
    Having a mental health disorder does not mean 'madness'. Unfortunately, this is what the vast majority of the general population associate with poor mental health and wellbeing. Buying into the stigma and perceiving the worst when you hear mental health disorder a) affects your perception of self (i.e. self-esteem issues) and b) may cause you to treat those with a mental health disorder negatively. Therefore, instead of buying into the stigma, buy into the fact that good mental health and wellbeing is about the

continual development of a positive state of mind. We may be at different stages here, but ultimately we should all strive to optimize our state of mind on a daily basis.

Remember, we all face daily challenges, and should therefore be more understanding when others struggle to cope with these. We can all play a role in creating a non-shameful atmosphere where those with a poor state of mind can admit it and seek support. Creating such an atmosphere will enable help be sought and given early, thereby preventing the development of a mental health disorder.

2. Deal with the root of the problem!
   We live in a society where there's a pill for most mental health disorders, and unfortunately that is often the first point of call. The problem with this is that you often just treat the symptoms and not the real problem. This leads to a never-ending cycle involving the use of medicines to maintain a positive state of mind. This also comes with all the other challenges involved in taking medicines. Thus a better and more lasting way of maintaining a positive state of mind is to identify the root cause of your problem. From there it will be easier for you to come up with a solution or coping mechanism for your unique situation. Similarly, if you are a carer or a friend or relative of someone struggling with mental health illness, use this principle to offer support or help.

3. Develop Resilience!

    Become resilient to your problem, that is, increase your ability to cope by changing your perspective. A pastor I know uses the acronym PMA, positive mental attitude, to encourage his congregation, and I think this is a good acronym to remember whenever you are facing challenges. There 'is power in positive thinking' and changing your perspective will enable you to become resilient to challenges you face.

4. Be Active!

    In the previous chapter on physical activity, the link between good physical health and physical activity was emphasized. Physical activity can have a profound effect on your mental health and wellbeing. This is a well-researched area, and the evidence for this is overwhelming. For instance, engaging in physical activity can decrease depression and anxiety. Depression in itself can quadruple your risk of developing heart disease, whilst anxiety can increase your risk of developing high blood pressure. Thus, by engaging in regular physical activities, you can improve your physical and mental wellbeing.

5. Keep Learning!

    Learning new things can provide you with a sense of achievement, which can also be a great pick up if you're feeling low. In addition, it can inspire you to take other active steps to improve your circumstances, which will inevitably improve your mental health and wellbeing. The important thing here is to commit to learning in steps; for example, read a book that inspires you or increases your awareness (not necessarily fiction as that's more for relaxation). Alternatively, do that course you have always wanted to do.

6. Hang out with Positive People!
I cannot emphasize this enough. Those you associate with have a profound effect on your mental state and approach to daily challenges. There is a popular saying that 'iron sharpens iron.' In other words, surround yourself with like-minded people and those you aspire to emulate. Remember, positive associations = PMA (positive mental attitude) and negative associations = NMA (negative mental attitude).

If you feel PMA is lacking in your social network then it may be time to change and join other groups comprising of people with similar interests as yourself and limiting (or eliminating in some cases!) your associations with people that lack PMA.

7. Stop Unhealthy Comparisons!
Comparisons can often bring feelings of inadequacies, depression and anxiety for the wrong reasons. Our life journeys and daily challenges are all different as are our perceptions of them. In reality, however your challenge is no greater than the person next to you and their challenge is no greater than yours. It is all to do with perception.

8. Spirituality

   Many of us believe in something. The power of spirituality and believing in something is often underestimated, but belief is an extremely powerful concept. Believing in something can give you hope, strength and the belief that you can rise above any challenge that comes your way. It helps you to focus on your abilities, your 'strengths' and 'what can be' not necessarily 'what is.' Indeed, it can give life more value and meaning, which is often lacking in those with poor mental states. On the other hand, spirituality can sometimes have a negative effect on mental wellbeing. It may encourage moral perfection and discourage engagement with relevant health institutions or compliance with advice given, worsening the mental state and sometimes physical health of individuals. Hence if you are a spiritual person, it is important to get the balance right and ensure it impacts on your mental wellbeing in a positive manner. This may depend on where you get your spiritual guidance from. In conclusion, remember that spirituality is about improving your life, and care should be exercised when taking on board any message that contradicts that principle or advises you to go against well-intended professional advice.

9. Go for It!

   Aim to achieve various set goals. This could be related to your health, career, house etc. it could even be something as simple as volunteering. Research has shown that giving of yourself also improves your mental wellbeing. Furthermore, setting and achieving goals will give you a sense of achievement and help you to improve your life and health simultaneously. This in turn will lead to a positive state of mind.

10. Relax and chill!

We discussed the importance of sleep and rest in the previous chapter. It also features here because with relaxation comes calmness and less anxiety. You are able to think better and be more productive, thereby improving your overall mental wellbeing.

It is important to be aware that although you may not always be able to get rid of the problem or challenge straight away, through carrying out any of the actions listed above you should be able to see beyond your problems and challenges, whilst focusing on your abilities and possibilities.

This should enable you to feel good and maintain a positive state of mind. This is important as it is unlikely that you will ever be able to solve all your problems at the same time. Nevertheless, you can develop resilience and your own unique coping mechanisms.

REFERENCES:

1. www.hse.gov.uk
2. World Health Organisation (WHO). Fact sheet for mental health: strengthening our response. Updated April 2016.
3. Simon Dein. British Medical Journal, Aug 1997. ABC of mental

MENTAL HEALTH AND WELLBEING

health. Mental health in a multi ethnic society. BMJ 1997; 315: 473. Doi: http//dx.doi.org/10.1136/bmj.315.7106.473.

4. Hollander A, Dal H, Lewis G et al. British Medical Journal, Mar 2016. Refugee migration and risk of schizophrenia and other non-affective psychoses: Cohort study of 1.3 million people in Sweden. BMJ 2016; 352: i1030. Doi: http/dx.doi. org/10.1136/bmj.

5. Mermot MG, Stansfield S, Patel C et al. The Lancet, June 1991. Health inequalities amongst British civil servants: The Whitehall II study. Lancet 1991; 337(8754): 1387- 1393.

6. Chang S, Stuckler D, Yip P, et al. British Medical Journal, Sept 2013. Impact of 2008 global economic crises in suicide: Time trend study in 54 countries. BMJ 2013; 347: f5239. Doi: http:// dx.doi.org/10.1136/bmj.

7. Mental Health Network, NHS Confederation. Factsheet, 2016 update. Key facts and trends in mental health.

6

SOCIAL WELLBEING
'CULTURE, RELATIONSHIPS AND HEALTH'

"Alone We Can Do So Little,
Together We Can Do So Much."
— Helen Keller

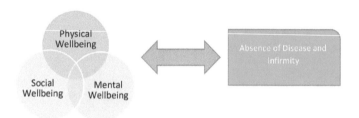

You may be wondering what 'social' has got to do with health. I must admit, this was something that intrigued me as well when I started learning about health from a wider perspective than taught in school. However, I've since learned about just how important it is, not just to the health of an individual but also the health and wellbeing of their community. Herein lays the difference between the 'social' and the 'other' elements of health, especially mental health, although there are strong similarities- social wellbeing refers to health from a community perspective. It's about healthy relationships with others in your 'community' or network. Being a part of a community and network with healthy relationships gives people a sense of belonging and involvement, which are vital for existence.

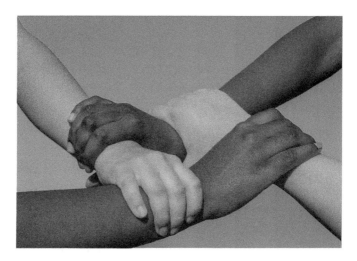

Figure 5. Together- Health and Wellbeing through Unity
Image from iStock

Although the term 'social wellbeing' may be relatively new, its definition is not. I'm sure you don't need a book to tell you that having positive relationships makes you feel good. This is because having a sense of belonging and feeling accepted is a basic human need. It is the reason why you go out of your way to be with or avoid certain people. Indeed, it is the reason why some people fight tooth and nail or commit to unimaginable tasks to join gangs, fraternities, 'boy clubs', etc. In such cases, people yearn to be accepted into a group or network that gives them a sense of importance and access to certain privileges. On the other hand, people that are unable to build positive relationships end up lacking a sense of belonging and consequently feeling lonely, which in itself can lead to depression. Notice the key link here: 'positive' not 'negative' relationships are what improves social wellbeing.

Increasingly, this is being recognized as a vital part of not just an individual's health but community health as a whole with the UK's faculty for public health describing it as the antidote to racism, stigma, violence and crime.[1] In fact, such is its popularity in health circles now that the UK's National Institute for Health and Care Excellence (NICE) calls it a necessary driver for healthy behaviours, which manifests on the back of good relationships with others.[2] Social wellbeing provides personal competencies such as emotional resilience, self-esteem and interpersonal skills, which all represent building blocks for personal development.[2] You see, many of the prominent issues we face in society are a symptom of bad social health. This is made worse because many children grow up with electronic devices as their best friends and lack the ability to foster positive relationships. Being able to build positive relationships is a skill that requires development like any other skill. Racism, stigma and crime all exist as a result of some people's inability to build and manage relationships positively.

At this stage I'm sure you're wondering, how does this affect my own personal health and well-being?

Well, some of the more personal benefits of forming healthy relationships with others within your community or network include:

1. Having a sense of belonging
2. An increase in your productivity
3. Getting and maintaining a positive state of mind. (Think about times when you've heard an encouraging word from a friend or family member, or even felt supported by a group)

Social wellbeing stands out from all the other components of health as it is not individualistic in nature. Rather, it highlights the fact that you need others just as much as others need you for your health and wellbeing. Yes, we need each other, and the moral here is we need to be more sensitive to the impact we have on others and their impact on us.

So, the next question you must be asking is how can I improve my social health and wellbeing?

The answer is simple, by addressing the factors that influence it in the first place. Depending on where you look, there are a number of them, this is my own personal list derived from a variety of sources.[1, 3.]

MENTAL WELLBEING OF YOUR ASSOCIATES

Have you ever heard the statement, "show me your friends and I'll show you who you are"? This is true as the individual mental wellbeing of those you associate with will impact on yours. Essentially, if you hang around sad people, it is likely you will be sad. Similarly, if you associate with happy people you are more likely to be happy. If you don't believe me, try hanging around someone that complains all the time and see how you feel compared to being with someone who makes light of bad situations!

YOUR LEADERS

Who are you subject to? This could be in your workplace, school, place of worship, local authority or country. It could also mean a mentor or personal coach. People underestimate the power they have as a follower. You have the power to choose who leads you in all spheres of life. Obviously, if you live in an authoritarian country such as China this power maybe somewhat limited; however, even then the government still needs people to buy into their ideals in order for them to lead them. The question to ask here is whether or not the leaders you have in your life are doing right by you and your community. Are they introducing policies that are relevant to the issues affecting you and your health? This is at the heart of social health and wellbeing.

We are fortunate to be living in a society and era where *in many cases* you can choose who you subject yourself to. Therefore, be sure to choose who governs, pastors or directs you with wisdom. Remember your leaders need you to follow them for them to be leaders, so hold them accountable because ultimately their actions will affect your health and wellbeing.

GAINING ACCESS TO THE RIGHT SERVICES AND SUPPORT

Accessing the right services and support when needed is somewhat dependent on resources such as your income and literacy level. This is why it is important to develop a learning and progressive mentality. Interestingly enough, we now know that poor health is largely a consequence of social inequalities as literacy is associated with healthier lifestyles. This is partly because increased literacy is associated with increased income, hence the ability to afford access to the right health services. However, being literate isn't necessarily about amassing qualifications. Thanks to technology, a wide variety of information is freely available online meaning that there is no excuse not to keep learning and empowering yourself to grow in knowledge. Buying and reading this book is a step in the right direction, but don't let this be the only action you take in the year ahead. Always think about what you can do better to improve your health and wellbeing. In so doing you'll also learn how to access the services and support you require.

RELATIONSHIPS WITHIN SOCIAL NETWORKS

Refer back to the previous chapter regarding the importance of positive 'associations.' The key point to remember is that not all relationships are healthy or encourage healthy behaviours. For those that do, there is evidence indicating positive ties can reduce the rate of progression of chronic diseases such as cancer and HIV.[3] You are also less prone to mental health disorders such as anxiety and depression.[3] This is partly because such ties are likely to encourage compliance with medications and support your coping mechanisms.

CULTURE AND SOCIAL NORMS, THE CONNECTION WITH HEALTH AND WELLBEING

Culture is probably one of the strongest of all the factors listed here; however, it is often overlooked and is an area the health community needs to pay more attention to because its impact on health and wellbeing is phenomenal. To highlight its relevance to health, let us take a quick walk down memory lane. My good friend Wikipedia defines culture as the sum of the attitudes, customs and beliefs that pertain to a group of people. It is often passed down from generation to generation and leads to stereotypical actions and behaviours amongst certain groups of people. It also has a massive influence on our beliefs.

Culture impacts on health as our ideas about health, and what it means to be healthy varies according to different cultures. For example, amongst the Efik tribe in Nigeria, there is a belief that a woman's size and fatness is linked to her beauty and wellbeing. Such is the strength of this belief that before a woman gets married she is sent to a 'fattening' room to be 'fattened' up for her husband! By contrast, in the West the goal is to be as slim as possible. Popular culture has evolved such that a woman's beauty is strongly linked to her size and the skinnier she is (even if she looks like a heroin addict!) the more beautiful she is considered. In both cases, as beauty is often associated with health, the culture indirectly influences the food intake, hence size and health of the woman in question. Now, the impact doesn't stop there. It is far reaching, and we all partake in behaviour that reflects the culture of the social network we belong to.[4] This could be the culture of the organization you work for or the profession or religion you belong to. Often you may not even be aware of this until you are faced with a 'foreign' culture with different practices from yours.

Making yourself aware of the cultures and 'norms' that shape your habits, whilst analyzing their benefits and risks, will enable you to adapt your behaviours to ensure they are healthy and agree with your current way of life and culture. Let me break it down further......

Currently, most of the health interventions used in health settings are utilized on the basis of evidence based medicine (EBM). This basically means using interventions that have been tried and tested under perfect conditions before getting to you. This is great in one sense as it enables us to ensure your medicines and other treatment interventions are developed under the best conditions possible. However, the downside of this is that the interventions are not linked to culture. Therefore, we have no idea of how effective a number of these interventions are at a societal level, which is often under less than perfect social conditions. Thus the onus is on health care practitioners to be aware of the need to adapt these interventions to suit various cultures. However, they can only do this if they (and more importantly, you) are aware of the cultures influencing your behaviours. For example, if Patient A informs his pharmacist that he is unable to take a particular medication with food in the afternoon because he fasts on a regular basis, the pharmacist may be able to suggest an alternative drug that is not required to be eaten with food or suggest an alternative time to take it. Another example could be illustrated with Lady B who belongs to a religion that believes her body should be covered at all times, except in the presence of her husband. Such a lady is automatically likely to be less exposed to sunlight and vitamin D (obtained from exposure to sunlight) putting her at high risk of bone disorders like osteoporosis in the long term. By being aware of this and discussing it with a health care professional, advice and support can be offered in order for her to get her vitamin D from alternative sources.

To finish off this section, I would like to give you a small assignment. Think about and list some of the key cultural norms that shape you and think about what impact they have on your health and wellbeing.

SOCIETAL NORMS

This is closely linked to culture, but is more of an expected pattern of behaviour where an individual is expected to conform to the relevant culture within a community. A good example of this is age, where lifestyles in the West are largely biased towards provision for young people, sometimes to the detriment of elderly people. It is often the case that several elderly people with multiple diseases can struggle to get the care and supervision they need, even in care homes, as these facilities don't always have or provide the right level of care. Consequently, this can lead to feelings of loneliness and poor life satisfaction. Subsequently, as a result of poor social wellbeing, their physical health and mental health deteriorate. This may result in premature death. On the other hand, in societies where the elderly are more valued, we see the reverse, especially where they are more socially engaged. For example, despite all the health challenges in Africa, available evidence suggests on average the elderly live longer.[5] This is probably because of a range of factors including strong social networks, with many elderly people being involved in various social activities. This confers a strong sense of belonging, in addition to the other benefits gained such as psychological wellbeing, life satisfaction and improved self-esteem.

So, to summarize although social wellbeing is less individualistic in comparison to the others it is just as important. By understanding and being aware of the cultures and societal norms shaping you, you can question and adapt certain behaviours uniquely. Central to this should be you exercising more control over your social wellbeing. This starts by going to places where you feel able to partake in activities as well as feeling valued with a sense of belonging.

REFERENCES:

1. The UK's Faculty of Public Health. Concepts of Mental and Social Wellbeing. www.fph.org.uk. Accessed November 2016.
2. National Institute for Health and Care Excellence (NICE). Local Government Briefing (LGB12), 2013. Social and Emotional Wellbeing for Children and Young People. September 2013.
3. Howell J, Koudenburg H, Loschelder D et al. European Journal of Social Psychology, Oct 2014. Happy but unhealthy: The relationship between social ties and health in an emerging network. Eur J. Soc. Psychol, 2014; 44(6): 612- 621. 10.1002/esjp.2030.
4. Napier D, Ancarno C, Butler B et al. The Lancet, Oct 2014. Lancet and University College of London Commission on Culture and Health, 2014; 384 (9954): 1607- 1639.
5. Kodzi I, Gyimah S, Emina J Et al. Ageing and Society, April 2011. Understanding ageing in Sub- Saharan Africa: Exploring the contributions of religious and secular social involvement to life satisfaction. Ageing Soc, 2011; 31(3): 455- 474. Doi: 10.1017/so144686x100010005.

PART 2

KEEPING DISEASE AT BAY

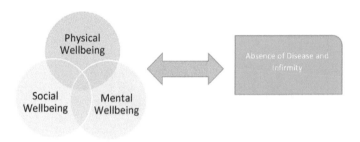

In the first part of this book we discussed physical, mental and social wellbeing, which all help to maintain good health whilst preventing the onset of disease. However, this is a very simplistic way of preventing diseases as working on your physical, mental and social health largely prevents non-infectious diseases such as heart disease, diabetes, cancer or depression etc. To look at health holistically and prevent diseases, one must also consider preventative measures for infectious diseases as well as key driving factors that influence our health behaviours.

Maintaining physical, mental and social wellbeing has no real impact on infectious diseases because infections are caused by the transfer of bugs between people or from animals by air, food, water or blood and other body fluids. Hence, the key to prevention here is to stop bugs from getting into your body and multiplying. In the following sections we will discuss how you can keep infections at bay.

Similarly, people often fall short of their health goals because they forget to consider key factors influencing their 'health' behaviours. These are vast and many, but for the sake of space, I have addressed a precious few that I believe can serve as a useful starting point.

7

THE POWER OF VACCINES

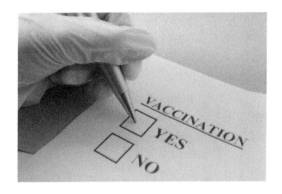

This has been a question that many have asked since the conception of modern-day vaccination in the 18th century by Edward Jenner. Using pus from a cowpox lesion on a milkmaid's hand he successfully vaccinated an 8-year-old boy against smallpox (the human version of cowpox).[2, 8] Jenner's experiments led to numerous awards and widespread vaccination, which resulted in dramatic decreases in smallpox occurrences in Europe and the United States. Given this was prior to the establishment of the link between disease and microorganisms (pre-germ theory era) contamination wasn't considered. This meant diseases like syphilis were easily spread as existing microbes were transferred from arm to arm during vaccination.[8]

Consequently, during the 1830s the anti-vaccination movement arose. The movement protested against compulsory vaccination, which it felt was an intrusion of privacy and bodily integrity.[8]

Fast-forward to the 20th century and you have an anti-vaccination movement able to generate controversy by the mere touch of a button. This is thanks to modern and social media. Consequently, recent decades have seen reduced uptake of vaccinations. Key examples of subsequent controversial cases are as follows[9]:

1930 – In Germany, a contaminated BCG (oral bacillus Calmette-Guerin) vaccine led to 256 babies getting tuberculosis, resulting in 76 deaths.

1976 – In the US, an influenza vaccine campaign led to a fifth of the population being vaccinated with 500 cases of Guillian–Barré syndrome (a neurological disease which can lead to muscle weakness and paralysis), resulting in 25 deaths.

2007 – In France, a study linking the hepatitis B vaccine to multiple sclerosis led to a 30% drop in its uptake.

2003 – In northen Nigeria, religious leaders suggested the polio vaccine was contaminated. Consequently, a mass immunization campaign was suspended. Inevitably this led to an increase in poliomyelitis cases. In addition, a subsequent increase in poliomyelitis associated with travellers led to reoccurrences in countries where the disease had been eliminated.

Of course, a really popular one that made headlines in the UK and across the globe was the MMR (measles, mumps and rubella) vaccine. Fuelled by a study published in the reputable medical journal, The Lancet in 1998, linking it with autism; this story is a sad example of what happens when bad ethics gets in the way of science.[1,2] It was a story that caused long-lasting effects that persist to date. It led to a significant drop in vaccination rates from 92% in 1995/96 to less than 80% by 2003.[9] The effect rippled across the globe and ever since there have been periodic outbreaks of measles across the globe.

The issues around this incident are worthy of a book in itself as the initial study started with lawyers trying to cook up evidence to support a massive lawsuit against the MMR vaccine manufacturers.[10] To be fair to Wakefield (the paper's author), his initial paper only *suggested* a link and stated that more work was needed to prove this.[10] Unfortunately, as with many such cases, many people interpreted the link with autism conclusively and this is what went viral. Things got worse when, a few years later, he published papers questioning the safety of the entire immunization programme.[10] It later became apparent that Wakefield had received almost half a million pounds from lawyers to provide evidence to help them win their case.[10] This was prior to his initial paper. He also geared himself up to make extra 'bucks' through creating and selling autism-related diagnostic equipment.[10] Consequently, the GMC (general medical council) struck Wakefield off for manipulating data and an unethical code of conduct. The Lancet also retracted his initial paper.

Unfortunately, the damage had been done, and has subsequently led to many across the globe suffering unnecessary consequences. For example, a recent outbreak in 2014 reported 600 cases of measles in the States, where the disease had previously been eradicated.[11] A national survey there also reported that a third of adults still believe it is linked to autism.[11] This is in spite of a series of other more reliable studies showing no link with autism since the retracted study.

The United States has also experienced much controversy around vaccinations and their components. For example, the use of a mercury-containing preservative called thimerosal has also been linked to autism, attention deficit hyperactive disorder (ADHD) and developmental delays.[2] However, the evidence here is also inconclusive, especially with the quantities used in vaccines.[2, 3] In both cases, I feel these controversies are somewhat indicative of the power of the anti-vaccination movement supported by modern media's ability to sensationalize a story and have it go viral within seconds. Unfortunately, this has meant people don't get the full truth about vaccinations and consequently make premature and detrimental decisions.

So what is the truth about vaccines?

They are a medical product used to stimulate active immunity against particular infections artificially. They represent one of the most important medical inventions in history and are regarded by some as a 'miracle product.' History suggests they've been around since 429 BC when a Greek historian named Thucydides observed that survivors of the smallpox plague in Athens did not become re-infected with the disease.[4] The Chinese are also believed to have practised a primitive form of vaccination known as 'variolation,' which involved inserting powdered scabs from smallpox pustules up the noses of healthy individuals.[4]

Modern-day vaccines as we recognize them really started to become widely available and used globally in the 20th century. The truth of the matter is that, despite the conspiracy theories and alleged links with various conditions, they are still responsible for preventing more deaths worldwide than any other medical product, and there are several infections that many of us will never have to deal with courtesy of their existence. You see, vaccines prevent infectious diseases on a long-term basis, many of which are transmissible. This in turn prevents associated disabilities, illnesses and deaths. In fact a whopping 2.5 million deaths are prevented annually as a direct result of immunization (use of vaccines), and this doesn't include the number of associated disabilities and illnesses prevented in the absence of death.[5] In addition, they are often manufactured to limit the impact of serious infections like Ebola. However, don't just take it from me… let us look at some numbers to illustrate this fact.

 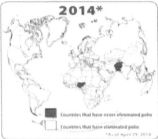

Figure 7. Illustration of progress against polio over a 26 year period
Image from CDC.gov, the official website of the Center for
Disease Control and Prevention

Many of you have probably received the polio vaccine, but probably don't appreciate the nature of the disease itself. It is an infectious disease caused by a bug that invades the nervous system to cause muscular paralysis, which leads to significant physical impairments and disabilities. Fortunately, as a direct result of vaccinations, this disease is now on the verge of global eradication, with only a handful of cases reported worldwide by WHO (mainly in Pakistan and Afghanistan) in recent years.

Quite simply, the numbers speak for themselves and as far as vaccines go, the good definitely outweighs the bad.

So, how does this 'miracle product' work?

Vaccines stimulate your immune system artificially to produce antibodies that act as 'soldiers' in the body as they defend against infections. A vaccine normally has a little of a particular bug (antigen) in it that is just enough to stimulate production of specific 'soldiers' (antibodies) against it.

The antigen may be non-living or living in nature. If it is living then it is usually modified so it is non-toxic; however, because of its nature it can cause mild symptoms or, in a few cases, full-blown diseases. Once vaccinated, the 'soldiers' produced remain 'asleep' in the immune system's 'bank' until it is infected with that particular bug. When infected, the immune system recalls its 'soldier cells' to kill or weaken the bug or its agent such that it is unable to cause damage to the body by way of infection.

WHY VACCINES ARE IMPORTANT

We touched on this briefly above, but essentially they:

- Prevent several including life-threatening infections (e.g. flu, hepatitis, measles, rubella)
- Have helped ensure you never fall victim to smallpox or polio as vaccines have helped eliminate such diseases from most countries
- Enable you to travel with no fear of contracting life-threatening infections abroad.

Vaccines are vital in preventing the onset of severe infectious diseases. They do what good hygiene and sanitation can't. They guarantee long-term protection from several infectious diseases including those caused by viruses that can spread regardless of how clean you are. Another important thing to be aware of is that by getting vaccinated and increasing vaccination uptake in your community you are helping to ensure the bug is eliminated from your community. This helps protect those that can't have vaccines for various reasons, such as with AIDS or allergies.

WHAT VACCINES DO I NEED?

This mainly depends on your age, medical history and gender, or where you might be travelling to.

Generally speaking, most countries have a schedule for what vaccinations are required and when. This is especially applicable to children and your pediatrician or GP can help you keep a check on vaccines administered and subsequent due dates. Ideally you should also have your own record for reference purposes. If you are an adult, then generally speaking most vaccines are reserved for people in certain jobs (e.g., health care professionals), the elderly or those with particular lifestyles or conditions. You should discuss with a health care professional as to which ones are recommended for you.

An exception to this is when travelling abroad where the need depends on destination rather than individual risk factors. Many countries have a specific list of recommended vaccinations which may be required to gain entry into them (e.g. yellow fever). Hence remember to check what vaccinations are recommended for your destination country whenever you are travelling, even if you have previously lived in the said country. This is because immunity sometimes wears off, and with some vaccines you need to have 'boosters' to ensure they are still effective. Countries often tell you what vaccinations are recommended when you are applying for a visa. You can also pop into any pharmacy or travel clinic when planning your travels for vaccination advice.

ARE THEY SAFE?

When you look at the numbers in terms of those vaccinated and those that have reacted, the gap is so wide and the odds of having a reaction so small that from a risk–benefit analysis it is difficult to justify not giving them. For most vaccines side effects are often minor in nature and may include soreness, swellings or redness around the injection site. In a few cases, fevers, rashes and aches can occur. Many have likened this onset to the flu itself as, though non-severe, it can be quite distressing when it occurs. More serious side effects can include seizures, disabilities and full-blown allergic reactions. However, these are rare and definitely not the norm. Consider discussing any concerns you have around side effects specific to a particular vaccine with a health care professional.

To conclude, I think it is important to put things into perspective. The fact is, on balance, the occurrence of serious side effects, including death and disabilities, is so rare in comparison to the risks of abstinence such that it is difficult to justify abstinence in most cases.

REFERENCES:

1. Wakefield A, Muril SH, Anthony A et al. The Lancet, Feb 1998. Ileal Lymphoid- nodular Hyperplasia, Non-Specific Colitis and Pervasive Developmental Disorder in Children. Lancet, 1998; 351(9103): 637- 641. Doi: http//dx.doi.org/10.1016/ s0140-6736 (97) 11096.

2. www.historyofvaccines.org

3. World Health Organisation (WHO). 2016. Online Questions and Answers. What are some of the myths and facts about vaccination? March 2016.

4. The History of Vaccinations. www.nhs.uk/conditions/ vaccinations/pages/the-history-of-vaccination.aspx. Accessed November 2016.

5. World Health Organisation (WHO). 2012. Global Vaccination Action Plan 2011-2020.

6. Leask J, Chapman S, Robbins SC. Vaccine, April 2010. "All manner of ills": The features of serious diseases attributed to vaccination. Vaccine 2010; 28(17): 3066- 3070.

7. Angiolli R, Lopez S, Alossi A, et al. Critical Reviews in Oncology/ Haematology, June 2016. Ten years of HPV vaccines: State of art & controversies. CROH, 2016; 102: 65- 72. Doi: http:// dx.doi.org/10.1016/j.critrevonc.2016.03.020.

8. Stern A, Merkel H. Health Affairs, May- June 2005. The history of vaccines and immunization: Familiar patterns, new challenges. Health Aff, 2005; 24(3): 611- 621. Doi10.1377/ hltheff.2403.611.

9. Patrick Zuber, World Health Organisation (WHO). Expert Review Vaccines, June 2009. Global Safety of Vaccines: Strengthening Systems for Monitoring, Management and the Role of GACVS. Expert Rev Vaccines, 2009; 8(6): 705- 716.

10. MMR Vaccine Controversy. https://en.wikipedia.org/wiki/

MMR_vaccine_controversy. Last Updated December 2016. Accessed December 2016.

11. Stav Ziv. Newsweek, October 2015. Andrew Wakefield Father of the Anti- vaccine Movement Responds to Current Measles Outbreak for the First Time. http://europe. newsweek.com.

8

HYGIENE –
THE FORGOTTEN PREVENTION TOOL

I really believe hygiene has been largely neglected as an interventional tool in our search for perfect drugs and cures. Good hygiene is the single most cost-effective means of preventing infectious diseases with the potential to slash the number of serious infections occurring worldwide.[1]

Unfortunately as it doesn't sell papers and you can't sell it, it rarely gets a mention alongside other interventions. Sadly, increased use of antibiotics and improved living conditions have coincided with a decreased emphasis on infection preventative measures such as hygiene. This in some-way reflects the modern era's over-reliance on pharmaceuticals as a quick fix. Indeed, the consequences of preventable infections are vast because unlike many other medical challenges they cut across medical specialties; for example, statistics indicate preventable infections are responsible for around 15-20% of cancers globally, with some infections like HIV referred to as 'carcinogenic infections.[2]

Unfortunately, we now have the added problem of antimicrobial resistance that has primarily arisen as a result of decades of antibiotic misuse and a dwindling antibiotic production pipeline. This has been exacerbated further by societal changes such as an ageing population with an increased occurrence of long-term illnesses. Both of which contribute to a decrease in immunity.

Given infectious diseases account for three of the top ten causes of death worldwide and costs the NHS £30 billion every year, there is a need to take action individually and at a societal level.[11] Chest- and stomach-related infections, such as food poisoning, account for a significant proportion of these, and numerous 'sickies' in the workplace which also costs the economy.

Although older people, pregnant women or those that have long-term illnesses are more vulnerable to infections, we all need to play a role here. Some of us can be carriers of bugs, including resistant bugs, whilst feeling well within ourselves, and we can unknowingly pass them on to others who, as a result of their vulnerability, may develop a full-blown infection. This is why it is vital that we all practise good hygiene and minimize the use of antibiotics, except where essential.

Now, there are many drivers of the above issues and corresponding solutions that range from improved surveillance systems to improved regulations around usage and engagement with the pharmaceutical industry; however, as this is a book about you improving your health we will focus on individual actions you can take to ensure that you reduce you and your communities risk of infections.

Vaccination, which we spoke about in the previous chapter, is one of two key preventative measures that I believe are key long-term infection antidotes. The second one will be the focus of this chapter. It is also a proven, highly effective and cheap technique that has been around for centuries, it is called **HYGIENE** and is as important to preventing infections as nutrition and exercise is to your physical health.

WHAT DOES HYGIENE MEAN?

When most people hear the word hygiene they think cleanliness, but that is only a part of it. Hygiene refers to *all the conditions and practices* that help maintain health and prevent the spread of infections.[5] The bad news here is that some of the conditions and practises involved are the remit of the government (e.g. ensuring widespread access to clean water, over which you may have limited control over). However, the good news is that you can still keep infections at bay by choosing to maintain your own personal hygiene and that of your immediate environment through engaging in hygienic practises.

Let me break it down further by grouping it into personal, sexual, food and environmental hygiene.

Personal Hygiene

This includes the basics at a personal level. It is 'personal' because it is often based on habits and practises that have been ingrained in people from a young age, hence it doesn't mean the same thing to everyone.

From a health perspective it involves keeping your body and things that have close contact with your body clean. It involves thorough cleansing of different body parts with soap and water regularly. This is important not just in terms of preventing common skin infections but also infections like the super bug, MRSA (methicillin resistant *Staphylococcus aureus*) infection. This can be deadly if it breaches the skin barrier to enter the bloodstream. One study looking at the link between personal hygiene factors ranging from sharing of toiletries, bed linen, headphones and nail clippers, and infections showed that personal hygiene scores were significantly lower in patients that had MRSA detected on their skin.[4] This highlights the importance of not sharing personal items and making sure such items are cleaned and sterilized on a regular basis, especially if they are being used on you in a public setting, such as a hair salon.

I use the word 'regular' rather than daily as different parts of the body have different requirements. Generally speaking, you should have a shower and brush your teeth at least once a day (some would suggest twice a day, especially your teeth if you eat a lot of sweet or acidic substances). This should involve washing your genitals, behind your ears and under your armpits as well. I don't think it is necessary for you to buy fancy cleaning products for your genital area as they can affect the acid-base balance of the area, and, consequently increase your risks of infections in that area. Good old fashioned soap and water is usually sufficient. In terms of your ears, you should wash behind the ears and use a finger to wash the outer part of the ear avoiding the inner canal (or 'hole') before rinsing. Occasionally you can get a build-up of wax, which is nature's way of keeping your ear clean; however, too much of it can pose problems and feel uncomfortable, in such cases you can use olive oil or an ear wax remover (available from your local pharmacy) to soften and remove it.

Other body parts that require attention include your-Hands: Regular hand washing is a must! I'm sorry if it seems like I'm stating the obvious! But you'll be amazed at how often this is overlooked, despite the fact that your hands are the most exposed and used part of your body. It is a major carrier of bugs that can be transferred to other parts of your body and to other people. Hence, you need to wash them frequently and after any activity that could contaminate them, such as after cleaning a child that's just defecated, using the toilet or before and after handling food. If in doubt, wash them anyway using soap and water, which, if in scarce supply, can be replaced with alcohol rub, which is widely available in pocket sized containers. You'll be surprised at how much of a difference this can make in terms of acquiring infections with one study linking it to a 40% decrease in occurrence of stomach-related infections.[4] Remember to use a moisturizer after washing so your hands don't become dry and prone to other problems such as eczema.

Nails: Fingernails should be washed and cleaned every time you wash your hands. Manicures that don't involve adding false nails can also be a good way of taking care of your fingernails. Your toenails are obviously washed anytime you wash your feet, but are also worthy of regular pedicures where the cuticles are cleaned thoroughly and dead skin removed, which can help make the area less habitable for bugs.

Hair: This may differ according to your race. We all have natural oils (sebum) secreted from our scalps, which is nature's way of keeping our hair and scalp moisturized. However, the differences in the nature of our hair and the amount of sebum secreted means our requirements in terms of how frequently we need to wash our hair differs from race to race For instance, most Caucasians need to wash their hair daily to prevent excessive build-up of sebum, whereas those of African descent can get away with washing their hair once a week, or every fortnight. The important thing here is to keep the hair clean, so in cases where there has been exposure to chemicals (e.g. during swimming or times of excessive sweat [causes build-up of salts]) more frequent hair washing may be required.

Feet: Although you wash your feet when you have a shower, like your hands they can also become a carrier of bugs and source of infection if care is not taken. This is particularly the case in places where there is water or dampness (e.g. gyms and swimming pools). In such environments it is important to wear flip flops or slippers to protect your feet. You should also avoid walking barefoot outside.

Sexual Hygiene

This is a form of personal hygiene, but is worthy of its own section as when practised fully can help prevent several sexually transmitted infections (STIs) including chlamydia, gonorrhoea, syphilis, herpes, hepatitis B and C, HIV and HPV (human papilloma virus).

Sexual hygiene refers to all the practises and conditions that help maintain good sexual health and prevent the occurrence of sexually transmitted diseases, which continue to pose a significant public health challenge in many countries.

Although those considered at most high risk of STIs include men who have sex with men, young adults under the age of 25 and ethnic minorities, it is important for all of us to be aware of the need to practise good sexual hygiene because significant numbers of infections are also being reported among people outside these groups, especially those that live in urban areas such as London.[9] It is thought that this is due to an interplay between socioeconomic, behavioural and cultural factors.[9] Socioeconomic factors are outside the scope of this book, but we've touched on the other factors earlier in the book.

STIs are highly contagious and can occur in the absence of symptoms. The good news is that good sexual hygiene, hence good sexual behaviours, can prevent most STIs and their resulting consequences, which can range from infertility to arthritis, and a range of cancers.

An important STI is AIDS (acquired immunodeficiency syndrome). AIDS occurs when you contract at least one consequent infection that occurs as a direct result of a weakened immune system. Many people wrongly use the term interchangeably with HIV (human immunodeficiency virus), which is actually the causal virus. It is possible to have HIV without AIDS, but it isn't possible to have AIDS without HIV. It is worth mentioning here as it is responsible for one of the greatest pandemics in history, and certainly the greatest of this generation. According to UNAIDS, since it was discovered in 1981 over 75 million have been infected, and almost 40 million have died. Thousands are also infected on a daily basis despite this being the most medically advanced era in history. Unfortunately, despite us living in an era with far more 'medical weapons' at our disposal than was the case in previous pandemics, we have failed to overcome this pandemic. Yes we have made significant progress as few now contract the disease through non-sexual routes of transmission such as blood transfusions, mother-to-child transmission (via pregnancy or breastfeeding), or sharing unsterilized sharp instruments (e.g. needles). We also have drugs that treat and, in some cases, prevent the disease, but we still have a long, long way to go in terms of actually eliminating the disease. You see, the vast majority of people that get HIV now get it through sex! In other words, sex, whether between the same or different sexes, plays a large part in this pandemic and other STIs across the globe. Hence, the guaranteed way to avoid getting HIV or any other sexually transmitted diseases is to abstain 100% from sex. Now, except you are a priest or nun, it is unlikely that that is a reality for you (and many others alike), thus the next best, and I might add cheapest, option is to ensure you are 'sexually hygienic'.

Society has become overly reliant on drugs to treat and now prevent this disease, in some ways becoming a victim of the pharmaceutical industries success in its production line for HIV, on the flip side for STIs mostly treated with antibiotics quite the opposite is the case because a dwindling antibiotic pipeline coupled with a rise in antibiotic resistance means that in the future more of us will be predisposed to difficult-to-treat STIs, which in turn will increase our risks of contracting HIV (the risks increase once you have an STI), furthering the case for changes in sexual behaviours hence sexual hygiene. In the long term there is no substitute for this intervention in terms of preventing both STIs and HIV.

So, what does sexual hygiene and having good sexual behaviours entail? Here's what I consider a 'top ten' tip list that summarizes how to be sexually hygienic and maintain your sexual health.

Top ten sexual hygiene tips!

1. Practice safe sex: I know this is stating the obvious, but the condom is still the most effective means of prevention for most STIs; however, it must be used correctly and consistently. Also, bear in mind it may not prevent STIs transmitted through oral sex or bodily fluids.

2. Practice monogamy: Try to stick to one sex partner at a time and avoid multiple sexual encounters or casual sex, where possible

3. Avoid risky sex: Although good sex involves being adventurous, try not to be too adventurous in your efforts to have good sex as some practices such as anal or drug-fuelled sex sometimes referred to as 'chemsex' increase your risk of acquiring a sexually transmitted infection (STI), especially HIV.

4. Avoid oral sex if there are sores on your partner's mouth or vice versa as this can transfer an infection from the mouth to your genitalia or vice versa.

5. Ensure you are up to date with your vaccinations as vaccines like those for human papilloma virus (HPV)

and hepatitis B are proven to reduce your risk of developing associated cancers like cancers of the cervix, penis and liver.

6. If you ever suspect you have a sexually transmitted infection, be sure to present to a health professional as many of the symptoms are similar and timely access to treatment with partner notification (i.e., ensuring all those you've been involved with sexually are notified and treated) is key here.

7. Regular sexual health screens are vital and should be done yearly if you are sexually active, and every three months if engaging in risky sexual practices such as condomless or casual sex.

8. Include a HIV test as part of your sexual health screen test. It is also worth doing a test prior to embarking on a sexual relationship with someone and periodically in long-term relationships as the relationship dynamics may change. Fortunately, these tests are now widely available from the Internet, selected pharmacies such as Boots and Superdrug, your GP and sexual health clinics in your local hospital.

9. If you end up having casual sex or risky sex without precautions, be sure to visit your nearest sexual health clinic or A & E department as you may need to take HIV prevention drugs.

10. Abstain from sexual intercourse if you've been exposed to an STI, or suspect a sexual partner you once had sex with as having an STI (usually for a set period as advised by a health care professional).

Now, for completion I might add here that there is the added option of taking a drug currently only available online in the UK with ongoing debate as to whether it should be made available on the NHS. The drug can help reduce your risk of contracting HIV, but I must stress this would not protect you from other STIs, thus if your overall goal is to be disease free without any risks of side effects, your best option is to practise good sexual hygiene as this is your passport to good and sustainable sexual health.

Food Hygiene

This is about how you handle, prepare, cook and store food. Although it is often difficult to tell how food you purchase is handled or prepared when eating out, in most cases foodborne diseases are virtually 100% preventable, just by applying hygienic practises.[4] Estimates suggest many hospital infections and some deaths are preventable by simply preparing and cooking food properly or 'hygienically.' There are a number of measures that may be employed to avoid food poisoning. Key ones are discussed below.[4, 10, 12]

SPLASHING!

Avoid this in the kitchen when washing food items as water droplets harbouring bugs can travel significant distances in all directions. This is especially applicable when washing poultry, meat or fish. In addition, don't allow the water to drip onto other surfaces or food, and be sure to drain items properly before putting in the fridge or moving to different surfaces.

WELL DONE IS PREFERABLE!!

It is a good idea to make sure things like chicken, sausages and pork are well done and steaming hot throughout before serving to ensure no bugs survive to cause food poisoning.

FREEZING AND REFRIGERATING

These are essential preservation methods that many of us can't live without. However, there are some key points to remember when defrosting and using refrigerated food:

- Defrost meat/fish/chicken thoroughly before cooking. You can use a microwave if cooking immediately otherwise use the fridge for overnight defrosting to ensure the meat doesn't get too warm and vulnerable to bug invasions.
- Once defrosted, avoid refreezing raw or cooked food.
- Heat food once after defrosting. Increased cooking and reheating increases the risk of food poisoning whilst decreasing its nutritional value.
- Aim to use all leftovers in the fridge within two days.

CLEANING SURFACES

Wash all worktops and chopping boards before and after cooking to avoid cross contamination. Also, wash surfaces (and utensils) in between uses for items such as meat, vegetables and fruit. Interestingly, the average kitchen chopping board is said to have around 200% more fecal bacteria on it than the average toilet seat!

MISCELLANEOUS ACTIONS

Other measures that may help you improve your food hygiene include:

* storing perishable foods (e.g. meat, vegetables and cooked food) in a refrigerator or freezer
* keeping raw and cooked foods separate
* washing food items before eating or cooking them
* avoiding food handling in the presence of skin conditions involving infections or broken skin
* aiming to complete initial food preparation to intake within four hours
* aiming to eat just after cooking, as prolonged storage at room temperature favours bug multiplication
* cooling or heating food rapidly (placing food in shallow containers may help with cooling)

ENVIRONMENTAL HYGIENE

Environmental hygiene is about trying to keep your immediate environment clean and reduce your chances of getting bugs from your environment. The following tips will go a long way in maintaining hygiene in your immediate environment.

* Allow regular fresh air circulation, this is particularly important if in the presence of someone with a

respiratory infection such as the common cold or tuberculosis (TB). This is because recirculation of air is common in most places because of heaters and air-conditioners, which increases the potential for microbial accumulation or growth.[4] This is further exacerbated by the altered relative humidity of the air, which can also influence survival of the bugs.

- Handle and dispose of all sharp objects safely and carefully; take needles to a pharmacy for disposal

- Use clean water. If in a place where supply is limited, consider filtering, boiling or using bottled water.

- Empty bins on a regular basis and consider using the more hygienic foot operated bins.

- Always dry surfaces after cleaning, as bugs thrive in damp conditions.

- Launder clothing at 40 to 60°C, ideally with a bleach-containing product to ensure elimination of bugs from clothing and household linens.

- Wash or change cleaning aids such as sponges regularly as bugs can easily attach to them, in some cases disposable cleaning items may be better.

- Regularly clean shower trays, wash corners of baths and remove lime scale build-up to stop bugs from feeling at home in your bathroom.

- Endeavour to put the above into practise whilst maintaining a clean environment to keep bugs and infections at bay. This should help maintain your health and wellbeing further.

REFERENCES:

1. Curtis V, Schmidt O, Luby S et al. The Lancet Infectious Diseases, April 2011. Hygiene: New hopes, new horizons. Lancet Infect Dis, 2011; 11(4):312- 21. Doi: 10.1016/S1473-3099(10)70224-3.

2. Casper C, Fitzmaurice C.The Lancet Global Health, July 2016. Infection related cancers: Prioritising an important and eliminable contribution to the global health cancer burden. Lancet Glob Health, 2016; 4(9):e580- e581. Doi: http://dx.doi.org/10.1016/S2214-109X(16)30169-3.

3. Antonnson A,Wilson L,Kendall B et al.Australia & New Zealand Journal of Public Health, Oct 2015. Cancers in Australia 2010 attributable to infectious agents. Aust N Z J Public Health, 2015; 39(5): 446– 451. Doi:10.111/1753.6405.12445

4. Bloomfield S, Exner M, Fara G et al. International Scientific Forum on Home Hygiene. A report celebrating 10 years of the International Scientific Forum on Home Hygiene: The Global burden of hygiene related diseases. June 2009

5. www.who.int/topics/hygiene/en/

6. www.who.int/water_sanitation_health/hygiene/settings/hvchap8.pdf

7. Top Ten causes of Death. WHO Fact Sheet No 310. http://www.who.int/mediacentre/factsheets/fs310/en/.   Updated May 2014

8. WHO World Health Day Antimicrobial Resistance Technical Working Group. The WHO policy package to combat antimicrobial resistance- WHO bulletin, 2011.

9. Public Health England Health Protection Report. Infection Report,Vol. 10: 22. July 2016, republished October 2016.

10. Heymann D.Alpha Press,American Public Health Association. *Control of Communicable Diseases Manual.* 20th Edition, 2015.

11. National Institute for Health and Care Excellence (NICE). Antimicrobial Stewardship: changing risk related behaviours in the general population. NICE Guideline (NG63), January 2017. https://www.nice.org.uk/guidance/ng63. Accessed January 2017.

12. www.nhs.uk/livewell/homehygiene/pages/homehygienehub. aspx. Accessed December 2016.

9

ARE DRUGS AND SUPPLEMENTS A SHORT-CUT TO GOOD HEALTH?

Recent estimates suggest almost 50% of us use prescription drugs on a regular basis.[1] I suspect the figures would be much higher if one includes supplements, herbs and drugs bought over the counter.

This highlights how much of an essential role drugs play in our lives, and as a society we are increasingly reliant on them because we associate them with good health. Unfortunately, for many, they have become a short-cut to better health and even health care professionals are sometimes guilty of using them as an easy option to treat patients rather than pushing them to take more responsibility for their health. Now, don't get me wrong, drugs are great and are the cornerstone of modern medical practice; however, they are not the answer to any nation's health challenges.

Drugs, as you may know, are chemicals or substances that can have an impact on all types of diseases whether infectious or non-infectious. They affect the way your body or a part of it functions and are generally taken to:

1. Treat or cure a disease or its symptoms
2. Prevent disease
3. Optimize health
4. Provide a form of escapism or relaxation.

They can be broadly categorized as follows:

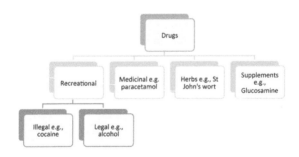

For the purpose of this book let us put recreational drugs to one side as they very rarely add any value to your health, often times they take away from it and are mainly used as a form of escapism hence the term 'recreational.' Instead, let us focus on the other three –

medicinal drugs, herbs and supplements. Medicinal drugs are what most people commonly associate with drugs used to treat disease. They are also used to prevent disease and cost the NHS billions each year. Two of the most frequently prescribed drugs – a statin (cholesterol lowering drug) and aspirin (a blood thinner that prevents heart attacks and strokes) are of the preventative type.[2] There is a lot to be said for preventative medicine, with significant evidence of societal and individual benefits within the context of an aging population. However, I am of the opinion that we need to avoid over-relying on medications, or supplements for that matter, to prevent disease onset. Rather, there should be more emphasis on supporting lifestyle changes. Every drug has side effects, some of which may require taking an additional tablet to prevent them. A good example here is aspirin, which can often cause stomach ulcers or bleeds for which we give a drug like lansoprazole to prevent. Lansoprazole, in turn, is linked to diarrhoea and dementia. You get the picture? This is the viscous cycle that can occur when using drugs to treat disease. Hence, it is hard not to make a case for increased and sustained efforts to change, maintain and rely on a healthy lifestyle.

For this chapter, I would like to focus on supplements widely used by many to optimize health and prevent disease. Now, you may have thought that herbs and supplements are harmless natural products well it is time for a little news flash. Remember our definition of drugs being substances that affect the way our body or parts of it function? Well on that basis alone they qualify as drugs; furthermore, several medications used to treat disease have herb origins. However, they are not drugs in a conventional sense and there are many definitions floating around that help to explain what they are. The definition I like most comes from the United States Dietary Supplement Health Education Act (DSHEA) 1994, which defines a dietary supplement as *'a product (other than tobacco) that is intended to supplement the diet which bears or contains one or more of the following dietary ingredients: a vitamin, a mineral, a herb or other botanical, an amino acid, a dietary substance for use by man to supplement the diet by increasing the total daily intake, or a concentrate, metabolite, constituent, extract or combinations of these ingredients. It is intended for ingestion in pill, capsule, tablet or liquid form, is not represented for use as a conventional food or as the sole item of a meal or diet and is labelled as a dietary supplement.'*[3] This definition is a bit of a mouthful but is all inclusive, and covers the wide variety of supplement products in existence. The industry itself is worth millions in the UK and globally as a result of effective marketing campaigns, various health fads and health programmes that claim supplements have the power to improve our health, boost our vitality, limit signs of aging, extend our lives, and reduce the risk of chronic diseases such as cancer. However, it is important to be aware that they are, as the name suggests, *'supplements,'* and are not on their own intended to treat, prevent or cure any disease so beware of any such claims as they have not gone through the necessary regulatory processes to make any such claims. Indeed, there are many schools of thought around their true impact, with some people and health professionals advocating their use and others dismissing their potential. Scientifically, the evidence supporting their use and benefits is relatively weak as, unlike medications, there is no requirement for supplements to prove their worth prior to coming to market.

Now, although I don't consider myself a strong advocate of all supplements, I do believe they have a place in modern preventative medicine. In particular, there are many scenarios where they can make a huge difference to people's health. There are millions of people, my own mother included, who swear by some of them. For instance, my mother, like many people in their sixties, often complains of joint pain, and requested some supplements from me. I got her some glucosamine and chondroitin – part of the natural cartilage that acts as a cushion between the bones in a joint. This can reduce with age and arthritic conditions. Hence, many believe taking them as a supplement slows joint destruction and relieves pain by helping to maintain this cushion between the joints. However, the scientific evidence is stacked against their usage and the UK's National Institute for Health and Care Excellence (NICE) doesn't recommend them as there is no evidence showing additional benefits in users compared to non-users. However, in reality, I have seen many patients who swear by them and testify to the difference they feel when they stop using them.

Although, legally, they aren't classified as drugs, in practise we treat them as drugs because their legal status is often just a way for manufacturers to get round rigorous regulatory processes. Furthermore, some of them have very potent biological effects often interacting and interfering with the actions of licensed drugs. In fact a recent study linked almost 4% of hospital admissions to adverse effects arising from supplement interactions with other medicines or supplements.[7] This makes them unsafe in certain situations and they can in fact lead to life-threatening situations. A good example here is St John's Wort, a popular herbal remedy used for depression. It isn't licensed as a medicine and is widely available without medical advice. However, it is extremely potent (strong) and can interact with several drugs, to cause a life-threatening skin disorder called Steven–Johnsons syndrome, see picture below:

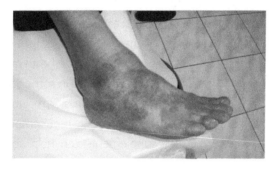

Figure 9. Picture showing a foot with Steven–Johnsons syndrome. Image taken from https://en.wikipedia.org/wiki/Cefaclor

Now, in all honesty I'm not sure this picture does justice to Steven–Johnsons syndrome. Having been involved in treating patients with it I have seen this disease (albeit severe cases) in real life. Believe me it isn't pretty as it can turn your whole body to an unrecognizable state. Patients affected require intense treatment as it is almost equivalent to being severely burnt with shedding of the skin and swelling of several body parts. Many times, patients end up being scarred for life. This, although an extreme example, is common place enough to highlight the need to exercise caution when dealing with supplements and seek advice in the following scenarios:

1. Combining supplements
2. Taking supplements with other drugs
3. Taking them instead of prescription medications
4. Taking too much or around the time of surgery

Now, a little bit about vitamins and minerals, which many presume to be safe and natural as they are often present in food. The truth about this is that our bodies only need small amounts of them to function properly. The best way to get enough is to eat a healthy diet. However, in some scenarios, such as when you are very young or old, sick, malnourished, pregnant or trying to conceive, your requirements may increase. In such cases, supplements can help you avoid deficiencies and the associated complications that can occur. Similarly, if you drink a lot of alcohol then you may be deficient in certain vitamins and minerals. This can make you prone to life-threatening conditions that can result in irreversible brain damage and ultimately death.

It is more difficult to justify regular use in the general population, especially those that are otherwise well and healthy. This is because the evidence that subtle deficiencies in several vitamins below levels causing classic deficiency syndromes, such as scurvy, are associated with chronic diseases such as cancer and osteoporosis is weak, with few if any randomized controlled trials.[4]

As yet there is no evidence that vitamins or minerals provide added benefits to a balanced and healthy diet for most individuals.[4] Part of the reason for this is we still don't know the various amounts of the different vitamins in our bodies before and after taking them, which makes it difficult to assess response to them on a general basis. Also, the evidence we have to date doesn't really tell us if the positive effects that occur in those that take regular supplements are due to the supplements or the healthy lifestyles that most people that take supplements engage in. However, it is important to be aware that this does not mean that there are no added benefits to taking supplements, and despite the lack of scientific evidence there is a case for taking some supplements or a regular multivitamin. This is because recent data from a national diet survey indicated:[5]

1. Less than a third of us eat five portions of fruit and vegetables per day.
2. Few of us eat the recommended weekly portion of oily fish (e.g. salmon, sardine, and mackerel).
3. Almost a third of women have low iron intake, which may translate to anaemic symptoms.
4. About 20% of adults are vitamin-D deficient.
5. Several of us have relatively low levels of potassium, magnesium and selenium.

Although it's difficult to decipher the health implications of this, it would suggest that a regular multivitamin would be useful for many. In addition, it is well known that intense farming practises (reliant on inorganic fertilisers), overuse of soil, manufacturing processes, the way we cook compared to years gone by may all contribute to decreasing the nutritional value of the foods we consume.[6]

It is important that whatever choice you make with regards taking supplements that you take a balanced diet rich in fruit and vegetables as we know that is definitely associated with a reduced risk of several chronic diseases such as cancer and heart disease. The reason for this is not just because such a diet is likely to be rich in minerals, vitamins and antioxidants. Rather, it's the fact that there are other less well-defined nutrients that co-exist with the latter in a manner that is difficult to replicate in a laboratory or pill. Furthermore, taking a diet rich in fruit and vegetables also entails taking adequate fibre and less fat. Thus, the take-home message here is that taking supplements does not replace the need to take adequate fruit and vegetables in your diet! Sorry to disappoint you if you've been replacing fruit and vegetables in your diet with supplements.

You may find it useful to ask yourself some questions prior to buying supplements or embarking on a lifetime journey with them and consider:

1. What does the product claim to do?
2. Is the product's claim substantiated with evidence from a reliable institution such as NICE, the Food Standard

Agency (FSA) in the UK or the Food and Drug Agency (FDA) in the US?

3. Is it from a reputable source?
4. Is it going to cause you any harm?
5. Is it worth the money? Consider a trial with and without to see if it makes any difference.
6. Are there alternative ways to get those supplements? (E.g. by improving your eating habits).

In conclusion, remember that although changing lifestyles and over processing of food may sometimes make it hard to get all the required nutrients from food (somewhat justifying regular supplementation), it does not in any way substitute the need for a balanced diet and that should always be your primary aim, wherever possible.

Useful Tips

1. *You don't need to eat fat-soluble vitamins (A, D, E, and K) daily as they accumulate in the body.*
2. *Steam, grill or even stir-fry vegetables to reduce loss of nutrients due to heat and leaching.*
3. *Retain any water you use to cook food containing water soluble vitamins to minimise losses.*

REFERENCES:

1. Scholes S, Faulding S, Mindell J. Health and Safety Executive, 2013. Use of Prescribed Medicines; 1:5.

2. Prescribing and Medicines Team Health and Social Care Information Centre, 2016. Prescription Cost Analyses-Prescriptions Dispensed in Community, England 2005- 2015; July 2016. www.hscic.gov.uk.

3. National Institutions of Health Office of Dietary Supplements. Dietary Supplement Health and Education Act of 1994. Public Law 103-417. 103rd Congress. https://ods.od.nih.gov.

4. Fairfield K. Vitamin Supplementation in Disease Prevention. www.uptodate.com. Updated March 2016. Accessed November 2016.

5. Public Health England and Food Standards Agency. 2014. Statistical Press Notice: National Diet and Nutritional Survey: Results from Years 5 & 6 (combined) of the Rolling Programme (2012/13- 2013/14). Update from Years 1-4 (2008/9- 2011/12); 2014.

6. Public Health England, McLance and Widdowson's. The Composition of Foods Integrated Dataset 2015. User Guide.

7. Levy I, Attias S, Ben-Ayre E et al. British Journal of Clinical Pharmacology, Nov 2016. Adverse events associated with dietary and herbal supplements among inpatients. BJCP Abstract, 2016. Doi: 10.1111/bcp.13158.

10

CANCER
– *CUTTING THE RISKS...*

One in two of you reading this book will be diagnosed with some form of cancer in your lifetime according to Cancer Research UK.[1] Pretty grim statistics, huh? Now, this is not a book about cancer and I could not do justice to the topic in a single chapter. However, taking the statistics into consideration, it is impossible to write a book about health without saying something about this disease.

For the benefit of those fortunate enough to have never been or known anyone affected by the disease, let me explain it simply in one sentence. It is uncontrolled growth of abnormal cells within your body due to changes within your DNA (i.e., your genetic blueprint). The consequences? Crowding out of normal cells, resulting in malfunctioning of body systems and various other symptoms causing significant discomfort and pain, which worsens with disease progression.

Cancer in itself is an extremely complex disease and although we still don't know the ins and outs of what causes it, we do know what increases its risks. We also know that occurrences are on the increase with a recent study highlighting a 33% increase in cases across the globe in the last decade.[12] The good news is that current estimates indicate almost half of all cancers are preventable because they are linked to factors you can control.[11] Obviously, in some cases, genetics play a massive role and there is a limit to what can be done in such cases. However, disease prevention generally entails addressing a number of risk factors with the aim of reducing overall risk. Hence for the remainder of this chapter we will focus on risk factors within your control.

The risk factors within your control can be broadly grouped as follows:

1. Lifestyle factors – alcohol, tobacco smoking, diet, physical inactivity and being overweight
2. Exposure to radiation through sunlight, x-rays, radiotherapy etc.
3. Infections caused by *Helicobacter pylori*, HPV (human papilloma virus), hepatitis B and C, etc.
4. Medical treatments like chemotherapy and immunosuppressants

5. Exposure to various chemicals such as those found in food, toiletries and the environment.

Now, let's take a look at each of these groups individually.

LIFESTYLE FACTORS

I won't dwell too much on tobacco and alcohol as there is hardly a day goes by that either of these substances is not on the news, and knowledge of their adverse effects is pretty widespread.

One of the things I do think is worth talking about is food. Yes, I know we touched on food earlier on in the book, but let us look at it from a 'cancer' point of view.

Did you know that being overweight or obese is estimated to cause 20% of cancers worldwide? Now, if ever there was case for losing or maintaining a healthy weight this has to be one of the strongest as breast, endometrial, ovarian, hepatocellular (liver) and colorectal cancer have all been linked to excess weight.[5, 6]

Now, as weight is directly related to physical activity and intake, let's expand a bit more on the dietary side of things. You may have heard that certain food items are good or bad for you as they increase or reduce your risk of cancer. Some of these claims are well founded; for example, there is some evidence to suggest that processed meat is carcinogenous (can cause cancer), but limited evidence to suggest the same for red meat.[5] Similarly, tomato products have been linked with a decreased incidence of prostate cancer.[5] However, such claims don't tell the whole picture and can be somewhat misleading as what is becoming more evident is the fact that it is dietary patterns that are important when it comes to long-term diseases such as cancer. In fact this has been illustrated with a number of studies pertaining to the Mediterranean diet (rich in fruit and vegetables, nuts, legumes, whole wheat bread, fish and olive oil) in recent years. For instance, one cohort study showed such diets to be associated with a 12% lower risk of cancer.[5] A larger analysis of the EPIC (European Prospective Investigation into Cancer and Nutrition Study) cohort involving over half a million participants showed similar results highlighting the link with a decreased risk of cancer.[7] Thus the take-home message here is to think about, and make changes to your entire diet rather than isolated changes such as extra tomatoes or less processed meat.

EXPOSURE TO RADIATION

Radiation, according to Wikipedia, is the transmission of energy in the form of waves or particles through space or a material medium. From a medical perspective this principle is utilized to target and kill off cancer cells during radiotherapy. It becomes a health problem when cells are inadvertently exposed to excessive amounts or for relatively long durations, an example being exposure via ultra violet light from the sun. Over time, the high energy generated through this can lead to mutations in DNA, which can cause the cell to die or become cancerous in later years. This often manifests as skin cancer. Other sources of radiation include investigative equipment such as x-rays and computed tomography (CT) scanners. Remember that such exposures are of a relatively low dose, and the benefits far outweigh the risks in majority of such cases.[9]

Now, it's important to recognize that you do need some sunlight exposure for the sake of vitamin D, but not the kind that involves long periods in the sun or using sun beds with the aim of tanning. If you do need to be in the sun, then the following tips may help minimize the amount of UV radiation you are exposed to: [13, 14]

1. Sunscreen: There are a wide range available and its best to seek advice from your local pharmacist as to the best option, bearing in mind that those with a sun protection factor (SPF) of 15 at the very least is what would be required for most people. Be sure to top up with adequate amounts regularly when in the sun, and try to limit your time in the sun to early morning before 11 a.m. or after 3 p.m. when UV rays are weakest.

2. Clothing: Darker coloured close-weave fabrics will ensure less vulnerability to the UV rays as they are less likely to penetrate the clothing to affect your skin. A wide brimmed hat will also afford protection to exposed parts of your body (e.g. face and arms) so you may find it helpful to invest in one of these.

3. Glasses: Wearing sunglasses will help to protect your eyes, especially those that cover the sides of the eyes where rays can often penetrate to affect the delicate skin surrounding your eyes.

4. Use Less if Darker Skinned: Generally speaking, the darker your skin the less vulnerable it is to UV rays, hence if you're an ethnic minority, then you only really need sunscreens during times of significant exposures.

5. Apply cream liberally and frequently when in the sun as it easily comes off.

For further, more specific, tips, you may find it helpful to speak to your local pharmacist before purchasing a sunscreen.

INFECTIOUS AGENTS

These are deemed to be responsible for around 20% of new cancers worldwide.[11] Common infection-related cancers include cancer of the liver, stomach and cervix.[5] Others include those linked to a range of viruses such as HIV and the human papilloma virus (HPV). Infection-related cancers highlight the need for you to ensure you do what you can to minimize your risk of infections as covered in the chapters on vaccination and hygiene.

MEDICAL TREATMENTS

There are a range of medical treatments from chemotherapy to radiotherapy, and other drugs that have been linked to cancer. However, these are outside the scope of this book as such treatments are often a last resort, and a comprehensive risk–benefit analysis is usually done prior to their use.

EXPOSURE TO VARIOUS CHEMICALS

We are exposed to a wide range of chemicals on a daily basis. Because of their vast number and occurrence, I've decided to exclude air or water pollutants. This is because such exposures can only really be tackled properly through effective government policies. Hence the focus here will be on chemical carcinogens (cancer causing substances or exposures) that you can control your exposure to and to which you are exposed to on a regular basis through food, consumer products and occupation.

Chemical exposures have been the subject of much debate ever since Doll and Peto released their landmark study in 1981. In the study they countered previous analysis by the US government to suggest occupational exposures to chemicals only accounted for 4% of cancer-related deaths as opposed to 20%.[18,20] They went further to suggest that majority of cancer-related deaths were due to lifestyle factors like smoking and poor diet. This study formed the basis for several estimates and global policies still in use today.[20] Doll, or Sir Richard Doll as he was known before his death in 2005, was well known worldwide in the scientific community and beyond for his contributions to public health. Many of these involved the use of statistics to deduce causal factors for cancer, tobacco smoking being one of the most well-known associations he deduced. Unfortunately, there are many that have suggested his landmark study and subsequent studies to do with chemical exposures may have been heavily influenced by his relationship with the chemical industry and consulting fees he received from the likes of Monsanto and other large chemical manufacturers that weren't declared and preceded the landmark study.[19, 21, 22]

Moving forward… Current research and evidence suggests that the link between chemical exposures and cancer may have been underestimated and somewhat trivialized. This has since led the US President's Cancer Panel to issue a national apology on the matter, where they concluded 'the widely quoted estimates of Doll & Peto were woefully out of date and that the true burden of environmentally induced cancer had been grossly underestimated.'[20]

Now, although most of the chemicals we're exposed to have undergone stringent testing to ensure they are safe to use, there is still a lot of uncertainty with regards their links to cancer in particular. Current research is starting to show that such chemicals even at relatively low doses may affect processes involved in cancer development (carcinogenesis), especially exposures to a combination of such. The UK's independent government advisory body on Mutagenicity of Chemicals in Food, Consumer Products and the Environment adds further weight to this by stating that "*it isn't possible to identify a minimum exposure below which permanent changes in your DNA ceases to occur and that even low-dose exposures can be associated with small increases in risk*."[17] Getting conclusive evidence around this is very challenging as exposure to a carcinogen (cancer causing agent), regardless of dose, doesn't automatically predispose one to cancer as an interplay of factors need to be considered from duration, amount, and intensity of the exposure through to the genetic make-up of an individual. Another factor that makes matters more complicated is that most of these tests are done on animals in controlled environments within laboratories, which represents a sharp contrast to the real world where you and I live. Furthermore, it is impossible for tests to mirror the effects of time as it can take several years between constant exposure to a carcinogen and the actual development of cancer.

When it comes to chemicals, there are known carcinogens that are directly linked to cancer, such as tobacco. For many of these there is clear guidance on when to avoid them completely or how to use them safely. However, there are substances that though not considered carcinogenic on their own may still have an indirect link to cancer. A recent study that made the headlines in 2015 was focused on this and highlighted some interesting points around the subject matter. The study was done as a systematic review and centred around the fact that there are a number of substances that, though not individually carcinogenic, are capable (at relatively low doses) of acting adversely on important cancer related mechanisms.[2]

It is important to note here that, although there is limited evidence to confirm the frequent suggestions made around carcinogenous substances in the media, it is difficult to dismiss these in their totality. Furthermore, this doesn't preclude you from taking a cautious or conscious approach to reduce your exposure to chemicals that may have the potential to increase your cancer risk. Remember, we are talking about risk reduction based on available knowledge and evidence.

In the reference study, after excluding direct carcinogens and those linked to lifestyle, they highlighted a range of commonly used chemicals in the environment that have the potential to affect carcinogenesis pathways. The key ones that grabbed my attention and tips on reducing your exposure to them are as follows:

1. Agricultural pesticides: These are substances used to kill or control living organisms of plant, animal or microbial origin that are considered to be pests. Most people are exposed through working with them e.g. farmers, or food intake. Previously linked to cancer and in the case of the reference study carcinogenesis, there is a case for limiting or reducing exposure where possible. Simple tips to help you reduce your exposure include:[10]
   - Washing fruit and vegetables under running water to help remove pesticide residues
   - Peeling the skin off fruit and vegetables can also help limit exposure; however, bear in mind the skin of some fruit and vegetables are nutritious in their own right.
   - Trimming the fat off meat, fish or poultry skin as they may retain pesticide residues.
   - Varying fruit and vegetable intake to minimize excessive exposure to a single pesticide.
2. Triclosan: An antimicrobial present in a range of personal care products from hand and body washes to toothpastes and cosmetics. This is gradually being phased out of use in most countries. It is banned in Europe, and was recently banned (September 2016)

from being used in over-the-counter antibacterial hand and body washes by the US FDA. The US ban was on the basis of limited evidence to suggest it was any better than regular soap and water and a lack of appropriate safety data regarding its use.[4] It is still permitted in toothpaste as there is evidence that it helps prevent gum disease.[4]

3. Bisphenol A (BPA): This is a plasticizer commonly used in food and drink packaging that can leach out into food or drink. It is also used as a lacquer to coat metal products like food cans, bottle tops and bottles. There is evidence from the Center for Disease Control and Prevention(CDC) in America that shows that non-intentional consumption enables a significant amount to find its way into our bodies; as a survey found detectable levels in 93% of 2517 urine samples of people over 6 years old![3] Closer to home, in Europe, the European Food Safety Authority states they don't believe BPA poses a health risk at levels the majority of us are exposed to.[25] However, they themselves admit there is a lot of uncertainty when it comes to specificities such that they recently reduced their recommended tolerable daily intake (TDI) levels.[25] This is a scenario where I think it would be wise to exercise some caution until any expert body can be conclusive either way. Tips that can help you limit your exposure are as follows:[3]

  • Leaching from containers is heat dependant, so avoid putting hot liquids or foods in such containers where possible.

- Avoid microwaving polycarbonate plastic food containers as, though strong and durable, over time and with high temperatures they can break down.
- Where possible, decrease use of canned foods.
- For hot food, aim to use glass, porcelain or stainless steel, wherever possible.

4. Nano-sized Particles: These are extremely tiny particles about 100,000 times smaller than the diameter of a single strand of human hair. They can't be seen with the naked eye, hence it is relatively easy for them to breech body barriers and gain passage into your body via ingestion, inhalation or even the skin.[3] They are often used in sunscreens, cosmetics, textiles, foods and paints, and use has increased consciously and passively by leakage from different objects in recent times.[2] Key examples include titanium dioxide and carbon-related fibrous nano particles.[2] Carbon related nano particles have also been shown to cause inflammation in the lung and linings of the kidney.[3]

5. Acrylamide: This is present in many homemade foods. It is formed by a chemical reaction at high temperatures when sugars (glucose/fructose) react with a free amino acid (asparagine), often in a low-moisture environment.[3,24] It occurs when food is fried, baked, roasted or toasted at high temperatures (over 120°C).[3,23] It contributes to the aroma, taste and colour of cooked foods. Having said this, it is important to put things into perspective here as cooking methods haven't really changed much over time. Hence it is fair to say we have always been exposed to some

acrylamide. However, exposure has increased in recent times as a result of its presence in several processed foods such as potato crisps, French fries, crispbread, ginger and breakfast biscuits amongst others.[24] Tips to reduce intake include:

- Aiming for a golden yellow color when frying, roasting, baking or toasting starchy food
- Frying food at lower temperatures
- Checking and following pack instructions when cooking packaged foods like 'chips'
- Not storing raw potatoes in the fridge (more free sugars form through 'cold sweetening')
- Soaking raw potato slices in water for 15-30 minutes before frying or roasting (ensure they are drained and blotted dry before cooking)
- Limiting intake of processed foods such as the examples given.

6. Phthalates: These are often used as plasticizers and in soaps, shampoos, hair sprays, nail polishes, food packaging and pharmaceuticals.[4] Similar to BPA, the CDC found relatively high levels of phthalates on a widespread basis in the US population when they did the National Health and Nutrition Examination Survey (NHANES 2003 to 2004) and looked at 13 different phthalates in over 2500 people aged 6 and over.[4, 5] Its link to adverse health effects is currently being questioned by regulatory authorities such as the MHRA and the FDA, but it was one of the chemicals associated with cancer development processes in the study.[2, 3,4]

As mentioned previously, the evidence linking chemical exposures to cancer is somewhat limited. Hence, an obsessive approach to avoiding all chemical exposures is probably uncalled for at the present time and is unrealistic. However, you may want to consider taking a cautious and considered approach towards minimizing exposure to these chemicals where at all possible. Remember, cancer prevention is about reducing overall risk and though there are no guarantees this will eliminate your chances of developing cancer, decreasing exposure won't do you any harm but may help to reduce your risks considerably.

To end the chapter, I'd like to give you a top-ten list of steps to summarize the chapter and help reduce your risks of cancer:

1. Maintain a healthy weight as obesity and being overweight is linked to some cancers.
2. Stop smoking (active or passive) as it has no known health benefits but clear links to cancer.
3. Limit your exposure to sun, and use sunscreen where exposure is unavoidable.
4. Limit alcohol intake to recommended levels and do not binge drink to make up for lost time.
5. Reduce your infection risks by being hygienic and accepting recommended vaccines.
6. Limit occupational risks by being vigilant and up to date with health and safety training.
7. Be aware of and heed warnings on toxic chemicals used at work or elsewhere.
8. Operate in well ventilated areas to minimize inhalation

of toxic fumes from various sources.

9. Minimize exposure, where possible, to chemicals directly or non-directly linked to cancer.

10. *Be sure to partake in national screening programmes for early detection of cancer.

*Note: Early detection is crucial in the fight to prevent cancer as this is when you have the most choice regarding treatment options and when it is most likely to be effective. In the UK, there is a national screening programme for cervical, breast and bowel cancer.[8] Depending on your age, you will be offered screening for all three if you are female but for just one (i.e., bowel cancer) if you are a man.[8]

Remember, be cautious but not obsessive in your approach as slow and steady often wins the race.

REFERENCES:

1. www.cancerresearchuk.org
2. Goodson III W, Lowe L, Carpenter D et al. Carcinogenesis, June 2015. Assessing the carcinogenic potential of low-dose exposures to chemical mixtures in the environment: The challenge ahead. Carcinogenesis, 2015; 36(1):S254- S296. Doi: https://doi.org/10.1093/carcin/bgv039.
3. National Institute of Environmental Health Sciences. US Department of Health and Human Services. www.niehs.nih. gov. Last Reviewed November 2016. Accessed December 2016.
4. United States Food and Drug Administration. www.fda.gov. Accessed December 2016.
5. Wolin K and Colditz G. Cancer Prevention. www.uptodate.

com. Last updated November 2016. Accessed December 2016.

6. Torre LA, Bray F, Siegel RF et al. Ca Cancer J Clin, March 2015. Global Cancer Statistics, 2012. 2015; 65(2): 87- 108. Doi: 10.3322/caac.21262. Epub 2015.

7. International Agency for Research on Cancer and World Health Organization. The EPIC Study. http://epic.iarc.fr/about/about.php. Accessed December 2016.

8. Cancer Screening. www.nhs.uk/livewell/preventing-cancer/pages/cancer-screening.aspx. Accessed December 2016.

9. The American Cancer Society. A Guide to Radiation Therapy. www.cancer.org. Accessed December 2016.

10. Pesticides and Food: Healthy, Sensible Food Practices. United States Environmental Protection Agency. https://www.epa.gov/safepestcontrol/pesticides-and-food-healthy-sensible-food-practices. Updated March 2016. Accessed December 2016

11. World Health Organisation (WHO). Cancer Fact Sheet, Number 297. Updated February 2015. Accessed December 2016

12. Fitzmaurice C, Allen C, Barber RM et al. Journal of American Medical Association for Oncology, April 2017. Global, Regional, and National Cancer Incidence, Mortality, Years of Life Lost, Years Lived With Disability, and Disability-Adjusted Life-years for 32 Cancer Groups, 1990 to 2015: A Systematic Analysis for the Global Burden of Disease Study. JAMA Oncol, 2017; 3(4): 524- 548. Doi: 10.1001/jamaoncol.2016.5688.

13. NHS Choices, Live Well. Sunscreen and Sun Safety. http://www.nhs.uk/Livewell/skin/Pages/Sunsafe.aspx. Last updated July 2016. Accessed December 2016.

14. Center for Disease Control. Sun Safety. https://www.cdc.gov/cancer. Last updated August 2016. Accessed December 2016.

15. Miller M, Goodson III W, Manjili M et al. Environmental Health Perspective, National Institute of Environmental Health Sciences, 2016. Low Dose Mixture Hypothesis of Carcinogenesis Workshop: Scientific Underpinnings and Research Recommendations. 12th August 2016. http://dx.doi.org/10.1289/EHP411.

16. Wild PC. Cancer Epidemiology Biomarkers and Prevention, Aug 2005. Complementing the Genome with an 'Exposome': The Outstanding Challenge of Environmental Exposure Measurement in Molecular Epidemiology. Cancer Epidemiol Biomarkers Prev, 2005; 14(8): 1847- 1850. Doi: 10.1158/1055-9965.EPI-05-0456.

17. Committee on Mutagenicity of Chemicals in Food, Consumer Products and the Environment (COM). Executive Summary, Guidance on the Significance of Chemical Induced Mutation for Human Health, June 2012.

18. Doll R and Peto R. Journal of National Cancer Institute, June 1981. The causes of cancer: Quantitative estimates of avoidable risks of cancer in the US Today (Abstract). J Natl Cancer Inst, 1981; 66(6): 1191- 308.

19. O'Neil R and Murray C. http://www.injurywatch.co.uk/news-and-groups/news/workplace-illness/exposed-workplace-cancer-naysayer-was-secretly-being-paid-by-drug-companies-231161138.

20. White M, Peipins L, Watson M et al. Journal of Adolescent Health, May 2013. Cancer prevention for the next generation. J Adolesc Health, 2013; 52(5 0): S1- S7. Doi: 10.1016/j.jadohealth.2013.02.016.

21. Tweedale G. International Journal of Occupational and Environmental Health, April 2007. Hero or Villain? Sir Richard Doll and Occupational Cancer. Int J Occup Environ Health, 2007; 13(2): 233- 235.

22. Hardell L, Walker M, Walhjalt B et al. American Journal of Industrial Medicine, March 2007. Secret ties to industry and conflicting interests in cancer research. Am J Ind Med, 2007; 50(3): 227- 233. Doi: 10.1002/ajim.20357.

23. Acrylamide. https://www.food.gov.uk/science/acrylamide-0. Accessed February 2017.

24. Food and Agricultural Organisation of the United Nations. Code of Practice for Reduction of Acrylamide in Foods. CAC/ RCP 67-2009. Adopted and Revised in 2009.

25. Bolognesi C, Castle L, Craved J. European Food Safety Authority (EFSA) Panel on Food Contact Materials, Enzymes, Flavourings and Processing Aids (CEF). Scientific Opinion on the risks to public health related to the presence of bisphenol A (BPA) in foodstuffs, January 2015; 13(1): 3978. Doi: 10.2903/j.efsa.2015.3978.

11

HEALTH THROUGH FAITH
– *CAN FAITH MAKE YOU WHOLE?*

"My people perish for lack of knowledge."–
Hosea 4 vs. 6, King James Bible

I put it to you that the vast majority of you reading this book believe in something. Am I right? If your answer is yes then this chapter is especially for you, and if it is no then read on anyway as you're about to see religion in a whole new light.

OK, that statement is actually based on fact as a certain place in America that engages in research around religion, the Pew Research Centre's forum on Religion and Public Life conducted a study across 230 countries and came to the conclusion that a whopping 84% of us belong to one of the five major religions – Christianity, Islam, Hinduism, Buddhism, or Folk religion.[1] This excludes all those that belong to the other 4199 religions in the world![1] Now, what this tells us is that the vast majority of us in the world identify with or are influenced by religion. Even if you don't consider yourself religious, you are likely to interact on a daily basis with those that consider themselves religious. Alternatively, you may interact with those exhibiting characteristics based on their religious upbringing courtesy of their home or school origins. Many societies' histories are built on the back of religion, from the Roman and British empires to modern-day America, Africa and the Middle East. It's a massive part of our fabric, which has been linked and continues to be linked to several conflicts and wars worldwide. Its influence on us, our behaviours and ultimately our health is tremendous, and many of us don't even realize it. Consequently, I have decided to devote this entire chapter to it.

So, I guess a good place to start will be with an explanation as to what religion actually means. For the purpose of this, let us refer to our good friend Wikipedia, which defines religion as

> "…*a cultural system of behaviours and practises such as rituals, prayers, sermons, world views, ethics and social organization that relate humanity to an order of existence.*"

Phew! What a mouthful! Now let us break it down a little more.

Generally, most religions pay reverence to a supreme being (order of existence) and herein lays the common thread between religions. Belief in this being or deity is not based on physical proof; rather, it is based on belief connected to religious belief. This is what many call faith; faith is about belief in the absence of proof. The interesting thing about faith is that we all exhibit it whether religious or not as we apply the principles in our daily life. In fact, having faith is very similar to what we call the 'placebo' effect in science, which is when a patient's symptoms improve significantly despite being given a drug that has no active ingredient in it. Several trials have been done around this, and the general consensus is that improvements are noted because of the power of perception and the fact that the person *expects* to improve. It is a wonderful illustration of the power of the human mind. However, despite being widely recognized in the science world it isn't relied on 100% because of its inconsistent effects and the unjustifiable ethics of choosing it over evidence-based options.

We also exhibit faith when we go to the doctor and listen to what they say or collect our drugs from the pharmacy and expect to get better. There is no proof that they are who they say they are, and that what is in the pill box is what they say is, yet we take their word for it because we trust in educational systems and relevant professional regulatory bodies to monitor their status and competencies.

FAITH, HEALTH AND WELLBEING – THE POSITIVES

To some extent, one could say faith as a principle is about expectation, but the key question is what do your beliefs say? What actions do they inspire you to take and what do they cause you to expect?

At this point you might be wondering how this relates to health and wellbeing, well let me explain. Religion has been shown not to just reduce death rates in the general population but also in many with chronic long-term diseases. For example, one review noted an association with religion and spirituality led to improvements in the clinical outcome of 76% of HIV patients.[2] In addition, a series of studies have shown religion and spirituality to be associated with improved physical, social and mental health outcomes (i.e., emotional wellbeing, anxiety, depression and general distress) in cancer patients.[3, 4, 5] This highlights its ability to improve all facets of health, thus improving health and wellbeing regardless of health status.

Religion or belief systems can help keep you healthy by serving as a coping resource to help you deal with adversity. This could be through providing you with a sense of purpose and control in various situations. This in turn can help keep mental health disorders like depression and anxiety at bay. In addition, being less stressed means you automatically improve your physical health by reducing your risk of developing conditions like hypertension and other resulting illnesses. Furthermore, the positive emotions you feel including happiness, hope and optimism means you are less likely to turn to drugs or alcohol to numb your emotional pain or hopelessness, which can and has, in many cases, resulted in chaotic and unhealthy lifestyles.

Also, remember, the behavioural system and ethics involved in practising religion; that is, the rules and regulations or doctrines governing many religions, helps encourage and ensure you support, respect and treat others in your social group with empathy, regardless of what they may be going through. This results in less chaos secondary to stressful situations such as divorce or sexually transmitted diseases etc. Similarly, you can expect to be treated fairly and not judged based on your health.

FAITH, HEALTH AND WELLBEING – THE NEGATIVES

On the flip side, however, religion is not without its faults when it comes to health; justifying negative behaviours, enabling negative emotions and war (which obviously don't do any good for one's health). It can cause some to feel inadequate as they adopt obsessive behaviours and attempt to reach unattainable standards often set by man in the name of religion. This can result in exclusion and isolation, which can put people at risk of adopting negative behaviours and lifestyles detrimental to their health. From a health-care perspective such doctrines often result in crucial delays in diagnoses, disregard of medical advice and/or rejection of medicines or medical interventions. Inevitably, in the long term, health suffers as diseases worsen to the point where they become more difficult to treat and, in some cases, the end result is premature death.

Unfortunately, the 'new age' churches don't help here as several pastors and religious institutions don't know how to communicate about illness. Many of them base their messages on faith and the belief that with faith no harm including illness, can come your way. They often fail to mention that, as with anything in life (including their messages of hope and prosperity), there are steps you need to take to achieve your health-related goals. These messages transcend to their congregations, who then feel unable to admit to suffering from a cold or even more severe illnesses such as HIV or mental health conditions. They fear that this is an acknowledgement of the 'devil's' power over them. This can result in crucial delays in seeking advice or help, which can mean the difference between living and dying. Some sicknesses, as has been discussed in previous chapters, are simply the result of living an unhealthy lifestyle. Please don't get me wrong here as I'm all for the message of hope, belief and inspiration provided by religious beliefs, without which there would be many more ill and dysfunctional people in the community. These messages are often progressive in nature and are vital to community (social) health and wellbeing, but churches and religious institutions also have a responsibility to be a source of motivation regarding health just like they are in other areas of life.

Another issue worth highlighting here is stigmatization of certain diseases due to the lack of knowledge and indifference of many religious institutions. In such scenarios, members of their congregations become ashamed to admit their struggle with disease compared to admitting their struggle with things like marital problems or a lack of prosperity. A good example here is HIV, which many in these institutions wrongly associate with promiscuity not realizing that there are a number of other ways it can be transmitted (e.g., blood transfusions or mother-to-child transmission). The point here is that diseases or infirmities are often caused by a variety of factors that require different interventions to 'heal' or treat them.

Now, one of the most common of these interventions is medicines, which have been used for thousands of years. They are referred to in the Bible on several occasions, such as in the book of Revelations where John the apostle describes a vision in which he saw "*trees of life with leaves that were used as medicines to heal nations.*"[7] Similarly, Ezekiel describes a vision where he sees leaves being used for healing, and the book of Isaiah refers to the manufacture of a medicinal ointment using figs to treat a boil.[7] Now some may refer to these as herbs in the natural sense of the word, but when you consider the fact that many modern day medicines originate from plant sources you start to realise that the use of medicines to heal and treat disease is not a modern phenomenon. Rather, it is an ancient practice that has been used from time. In fact one can argue that from a creational point of view it is a human essential up there with food and water, which were all provided by the creator. Possibly because the creator knew there would be times that our bodies would fail and need some external help to facilitate healing.

The point here is that medicines are ancient just as infirmities are, and churches would do well to realize this rather than shy away from talking to their congregations about health, and emphasizing the fact that being diagnosed with a disease and taking medicines doesn't make them any less 'religious' than any other member of the church. Remember, our bodies are like machines and can malfunction for a number of reasons. Thus, just as you would make an effort to correct a car or phone malfunction, in the same way you need to intervene when your body malfunctions. Similarly, it is also important to remember to take steps to prevent it from malfunctioning and to optimize its functionality where ever possible.

The Bible says, "*faith without works is dead*," (James 2:26) and that "*above all he wishes that we prosper and are in good health*," (3 John 1:2), why then would we expect to be free from disease without living healthy? Faith is as much about action as it is about belief, if you are a pastor reading this then just as you inspire your congregation to prosper to improve their lives, inspire them to live healthy and take the necessary steps involved, such as listening to the health care professionals in their life. Alternatively, if you are a regular church goer reading this, then respect your pastor and seek their spiritual advice to help improve your life as that's their job. Similarly, your doctor, nurse or pharmacist should be listened to when it comes to your health, as they are there to improve and maximize your health. Remember, our goals are the same – to see a better you!

I know some would say that they are believing God for a miracle as there are many examples of miracles in the Bible, this is true but fundamentally the point about miracles is no one can predict when one is going to occur (it is part of their beauty!). Indeed, in some cases, in the Bible people waited and suffered up to 40 years for a miraculous encounter. In such cases it is difficult to say wholeheartedly that such people wouldn't have benefited from some sort of medical intervention in the interim to help relieve some of the suffering they experienced.

Modern medicine may not have all the answers, but it definitely has some of the answers and, where possible, these should be applied until you get to the point where there are no more answers as that's when true miracles often occur. Alternatively, why not take the approach many men and women of God encourage you to take with other areas of life in terms of praying and committing your actions including medical interventions to God. This could be done with the belief that this will ultimately result in good health or successful healing of an ailment.

It is my personal opinion that if the church can get this right and really provide a true sense of hope and optimism with no shame in the face of disease then it can become a beacon of light and help tackle some of the greatest public health challenges of our time thus increasing its relevance in today's society.

To conclude, I think this chapter can be summed up by the words of one of the oldest women to grace the Guinness book of records, Gertrude Baines, who, born in 1894, as a direct descendant from slaves in Los Angeles was described as 'spry', cheerful and talkative'. When asked by a CNN correspondent back in 2009 at 114 years of age why she thought she'd lived so long, her answer was *'God, ask him. I took good care of myself, the way he wanted me to.'* Brief and to the point. Do your bit by honouring the body you've been given, and your belief will take care of the rest.

REFERENCES:

1. Pews Religious Centres Forum on Religion and Public Life. The Global Religious Landscape. December 2012
2. Doolitle B.R, Fiellin D.A, Justine A.C. AIDS and Behaviour, Dec 2016. Religion, spirituality and HIV clinical outcomes: A systematic review of the literature. AIDS Behav, 2016. Doi: 10.1007/s10461-016-1651-z.
3. Jim H.L, Pustejovsky J, Park C et al. Cancer, Nov 2015. Religion, spirituality and physical health in cancer patients: A meta-analysis. Cancer 2015; 121(21): 3760- 68. Doi: 10.1002/cncr.29353.
4. Salsman J, Pustejovsky J, Jim H et al. Cancer, Nov 2015. A meta-analytic approach to examining the correlation between religion or spirituality and mental health in cancer. Cancer 2015; 121(21): 3769- 78. Doi: 10.1002/cncr.29350.
5. Sherman A.C, Merluzzi T, Pustejovsky J et al. Cancer, Nov 2015. A meta-analytic review of religion or spiritual involvement and social health among cancer patients. Cancer 2015; 121(21): 3779- 88. Doi: 10.1002/cncr.29352.
6. Salsman J, Fitchett G, Merluzzi T. Cancer, Nov 2015. Religion, spirituality and health outcomes in cancer: A case for meta-analytic investigation. Cancer 2015; 121(21):3754- 59. Doi: 10.1002/cncr.29349.
7. Biblical References from the New Living Translation of the

Holy Bible, 2007. (Revelations 22:2, Ezekiel 47:12, Isaiah 38:21)

8.   CNN article –'114 Year Old Woman To Be the World's Oldest' http://edition.cnn.com/2009/WORLD/americas/01/03/ oldest.woman.gertrude.baines/index.html?iref=nextin

12

RISING ABOVE STRUGGLING HEALTH SYSTEMS

"Investing in knowledge pays the best interest."
— Benjamin Franklin

I've decided to include this chapter in this book because in the face of struggling health systems, I don't believe we can talk about improving your health without making personal investments in it.

For this chapter let us go back to basics! I will start by explaining what it means to invest. According to the Cambridge dictionary to invest is to put money, time or effort into something in order to get a profit, advantage or benefit. From this definition it is clear to see that we are all investors of some sort. The nature of what we invest tends to be age dependent. For example, as a student you might invest your time and effort in studying hard to get good results in the hope of gaining an advantage in the jobs market. As a professional you may invest time, money and effort in specialist courses in the hope that this accelerates your climb up the professional ladder. Alternatively, you may invest in a house in the hope that you are able to get a profit from it after a number of years or even so that you can live rent free in your later years. Health is no different, yet many of us fail to invest in it; yet how can you ensure you benefit from access to the health care you'll need in your latter years without making investments today to acquire those benefits?

Now, I admit the investments you make for your health will vary according to what country you live in as health is funded differently in different countries and some of you reading this may already be aware of the importance of setting aside money for this. However, for those of you that live in a country like the UK, with free access to health care services and treatments, or indeed those of you that have never made health investment a priority – this chapter is for you!

Founded in 1948, the UK's national health system (NHS) as recognized today is based on the underlying principle that 'good health care should be available to all based on clinical need and not ability to pay.' It is the world's largest publicly funded health service and is a source of envy to many across the globe.[8] Although its original focus weighed heavily towards diagnosis and treatment, its role in preventative health care has increased significantly since its early days of inception.

Over the years it has faced numerous challenges whilst trying to stay true to its founding principles. Recent years has seen it facing its biggest challenges since conception as investments into the NHS have dwindled on the back of significant debts. Pressures to save billions in the form of efficiency savings has also been exerted on it by the government. All this is in the face of an ever growing, ageing, informed and demanding population who want the best health care on offer. On this basis it is difficult to vouch for the continued existence and sustainability of the NHS in its current form. The reality is things are changing in the NHS, and accessing high-quality services, drugs and other treatments in a timely manner is likely to become more challenging in the years ahead.

However, it isn't just the NHS that's struggling, indeed around the world many health systems are struggling to do what they exist to do. You see, the goals of any good health system should be ensure good health and wellbeing amongst its population that is accessible and affordable by most through the efficient use of available resources. It should be able to promote, restore and maintain health as well as influence other factors directly or indirectly affecting health and health improvement activities. According to WHO it is all inclusive of organizations, people and actions whose primary intent is to promote, restore and maintain health.[6] This would entail private providers, health insurers, behavioural change programmes, social service providers and even a relative caring for a sick family member.

As with many other sectors in society, key to a health systems success is good governance and resources. Now, it is important to realize that resources are not just limited to finance as effective systems of management along with human and knowledge resources are also paramount. Cuba is a good illustration of this as they have managed to achieve significant health gains comparable to, and in some cases better than some industrialized countries. This has been in spite of significant political challenges and international trade embargoes on food, medicines and medical equipment.[15] This can somewhat be attributed to their sheer political will to survive in the face of adversity and more importantly, a heavy focus on preventative medicine.[15] Having said that, monetary investments and prioritization of health is still vital for health gains. For example, the Cuban Government prioritizes health expenditure as illustrated with a GDP of 11.1% for health compared to the UK's 9.1% and the US's 17.1%. This somewhat indicates a balance between reasonable investments and efficiencies within the system.[16]

It is important, and unfortunate, that many health systems try to look at and improve health in isolation from other sectors in society and the actual historical and cultural aspects of a society. Many are also rigid and slow in their approach towards effecting major changes, a good example being the recent Obamacare (affordable care) act in the States, which came into existence in 2012. Despite being hailed by many as one of the most ambitious and positive health reforms in the country's history, it was met with huge resistance from many.[7] Subsequent attempts to repeal it by the following administration highlights the difficulties and challenges involved in creating lasting changes to health care delivery.

Governance is a key issue, with many politicians often guilty of not stimulating honest debates around major changes for fear of electoral backlash. Another key issue is funding sources and resource allocation.

Most countries derive funding from general taxation (NHS), mandatory social health insurance (salary related), private health insurance, external sources (e.g. non-governmental organisations, loans from international banks) or personal health expenditures.[5] There is continual debate around the pros and cons of all these with regards achieving universal health coverage (i.e. widespread access to promotive, preventative, curative and rehabilitative health interventions at an affordable cost). However, it is largely agreed amongst policy experts globally that funding through general taxation or universal social insurance is preferable to alternatives such as private insurance.

This point was illustrated by a Commonwealth Fund report back in 2014. The report compared health systems in 10 countries including Australia, Canada, France, the US and the UK. The UK, funded through general taxation and a national insurance scheme, was declared the most impressive overall and rated highest in terms of safe, effective, co-ordinated and patient-centred care as well as efficiency.[9] It also had the least cost-related problems and was rated second in terms of access.[9] Not bad, don't you think? Especially when you consider the consistent negativity surrounding related debates in many quarters.

Despite the positives, current challenges are casting doubts on its sustainability in its current form. When one considers current economic pressures and political instabilities in Europe and beyond, recently fuelled by the Brexit vote, it is hard to predict the likely direct and indirect impact on health care largely funded through taxation. This implies there is a need for us to review the way health care is funded at an individual and societal level.

So, let's talk a bit about private health expenditures. Currently, this is largely based on personal health expenses rather than private health insurance in Europe and this in turn is often associated with poverty and significant strains on families.[5, 6] Although public expenditure is the main source of health expenditure in the UK, a sizeable proportion still stems from personal health expenses (~10%), with just under 3% coming from private medical insurance.[7] There is a case from a societal viewpoint for the government to consider subsidies in the form of tax relief (salary deductions before tax) or tax credits (deductions from your tax) to help support individuals to invest in their own health. This may help ease some of the pressure on the NHS. In addition, the government would do well to engage further with the health insurance industry to create products that would be mutually beneficial to the government, the industry, and most important of all the beneficiaries, you and me!

I think it is important for you to be aware of ongoing issues within the NHS as it affects us and our children. I do accept that there is a limit to how much we as individuals can influence the government's agenda. However, what we can do is improve and take ownership of our own individual health. This indeed was my objective in writing the book, so let us focus on what you can control or do at an individual level.

One of those things is personal budgetary allocations. The government has no control over this so you can invest your money as you see fit. Although, current issues would suggest there is wisdom in investing as a complement to what is freely available to you. This will help you rise above health system inefficiencies driven by ongoing pressures.

WHAT TO INVEST?

So, now we're clear on the need to invest, the next question you should ask is what should you invest?

I would say, to achieve your goal of maintaining and improving your health for today and tomorrow, you should invest effort, time and money. Now, effort is extremely important, but can't be measured so let us put it to one side for now and focus on what you can measure, which is time and money.

Time: This is about planning your life and day-to-day activities in such a way that you allow time for health-related activities. This could be time to get adequate rest or exercise (physical wellbeing), read a book (mental wellbeing) or time to socialize and mix with other people (social wellbeing). Essentially it is about allowing yourself time to apply the suggestions mentioned earlier in the book.

Money: This is a bit trickier as obviously some of the things mentioned above relate to money, but for the purpose of this book I mean real investments like the type of investments you make for a rainy day, such as car insurance or buying/building a house, which gives you security and enables you to take care of your today and tomorrow. From a health perspective this would usually entail some form of insurance or savings specifically for health related matters. There are a number of different ways you can invest your money, let me explain further.

PRIVATE HEALTH INSURANCE

According to Laing and Buisson, a company specializing in health care market intelligence research, only 11% of the UK population has some form of private health insurance.[1]

Now there are several reasons for this including age, with many in their 20s not giving it much thought, and those in their 30s and 40s just starting to appreciate its value. The message only really hits home when many get to their 50s and 60s, when they are at a high risk of developing a chronic disease if they haven't already got one. Unfortunately, by this time it is unaffordable for many and they end up having to rely on the NHS for everything, even it means significant delays due to pressures within the NHS.

In many respects private medical insurance may be advantageous for some, and this is recognized by the government. In fact it is the subject of ongoing discussions between the government and the insurance industry.[10] The difficulty here is that many insurance companies are risk averse as they often target those that can afford premiums, whilst having a low risk for developing a long-term illness. At times, they are also guilty of 'over treating' and over 'investigating'; for example, recently, a health corporation in America was indicted for fraud for performing unnecessary heart surgery for patients in Florida.[13]

There are conflicting views on the role of private medical insurance in the UK. Many policy experts frown on it as an option to lessen the NHS's burden on health care delivery. For instance, a recent independent commission wholeheartedly rejected new NHS charges and private insurance options on the basis that increased spending is affordable if phased in over a decade.[11] Similarly, international health policy expert Allyson Pollock believes that charges and private insurance will increase competition within the health sector and result in the less wealthy being left behind.[12] In reality, competition leads to winners and losers, and, in the case of the NHS, it would most likely be the loser because of increased pressures as it becomes overburdened with the poor and least healthy.

However, this isn't necessarily a balanced view of the current situation as private insurance is known to work in some situations such as when running complementary to the State, where it is made affordable with subsidies or when sold to groups rather than individuals as seen in Italy.[10] Furthermore, the present reality is that current taxes and NHS funding is inadequate to meet up with an ever growing and demanding public. There have been many unfortunate incidents, some of which I myself have witnessed as a direct result of ongoing challenges within the system. These are often based on staff shortages albeit not of managers; rather, of clinical staff and have led to poor care hence outcomes in patients. In some cases, I have seen patients leave hospital worse off than when they came in. I do accept however, that there is definitely room for the government to increase health spending. Especially when you consider our annual spend or GDP (9.1%) on health is significantly lower than in other countries such as our neighbours in France (11.5%), Cuba a developing country (11.1%) and the US (17.1%).[16] However, I doubt that alone will lead to major successes without a comprehensive overview of our approach to health care delivery at the present time. For example, practical measures (not just campaigns) to support employers to improve the health and wellbeing of their staff would go a long way in reducing pressures on the NHS.

Private medical insurance run complementary to the NHS is an option. However, for it to work effectively alongside the NHS there is a need for comprehensive government regulations and wider reaching products. As per recommendations in a recent department of health pensions and insurance working group, this could be in the form of coverage for extended age illnesses or whole-life insurance triggered by care needs rather than death.[10]

As discussions continue, and we hope for a mutually beneficial consensus between the government and the insurance industry, health insurance may well be worth considering on an individual basis. It may help you circumvent the NHS's shortfalls. It can enable you to fast track consultant appointments and avoid indefinite waiting lists for procedures such as hip replacement surgery. It may also enable you access evidence-based drugs yet to be approved by NICE, which makes decisions based on cost effectiveness and population rather than individual needs. Furthermore, it can help cater for the little things that contribute to your general wellbeing in times of health challenges such as complementary therapies or home nursing. However, there are some limitations as it may not cover unproven treatments, long-term illnesses, and drug abuse or kidney dialysis. There are, however, alternative methods of financing and catering for such diseases.[4] One of such methods is critical illness cover, which we will discuss later on.

Many health insurance options also cover several preventative interventions, which include thorough investigative screening at a range of private providers. Such screening although excessive at times can help prevent late diagnoses of several diseases as they may be picked up earlier. This can lead to earlier initiation of treatment when success is more likely.

How Does Private Health Insurance Work?

So now that we've spoken at length about the NHS and the potential benefits of health insurance, I'm sure many of you reading are now wondering what exactly private health insurance is all about and how it works. Well, you'll be pleased to know that I've devoted the rest of the chapter to this. I hope that whether or not you choose to go down the health insurance route, you will have a greater understanding of how it works and how to research the right product for yourself.

Health insurance can be quite complicated as getting the most out of it very much depends on where you reside and what is available within the health care system. In addition, unlike other types of insurance it is difficult to change on an annual basis as a result of the fact that premiums rise with age and most insurers won't cover pre-existing conditions. This means that when you develop an illness on your existing policy, your ability to get another policy becomes hindered.

Now, to understand health insurance in its fullness you must understand the basis of cover, which, in the UK in particular, relates to how much of your medical history you give to the insurer. There are two main forms of cover, they are:[2, 4]

1. Full Medical Underwriting – This is where you provide full details of your medical history, if you leave anything out then the insurer may refuse to pay out a claim at a future date. It is often the costlier of the two.
2. Moratorium Underwriting – This is where you are not asked to provide full details of your medical history as it excludes pre-existing conditions for which you have had symptoms, received treatment or medications for in the last 5 years, usually for a set period of 2 years after which they may be included.

From a policy point of view the options are vast as there are policies for individuals and their families, the self-employed, union or professional organization members, the list goes on. There are even options for those living or working abroad. Money doesn't have to be a barrier either as with options available for as low as £25 per month you can access cover worth thousands. It doesn't end there because within each policy there are a wide variety of offers, one size doesn't fit all, and things like affordability, need, lifestyle, age, occupation and family history will often determine which one is best for you. This is why it is helpful and beneficial to engage with a broker who can help advice and tailor a policy to suit your needs. Of course, this doesn't mean that you shouldn't do your own research and aim to get a range of quotes as you would do with most things.

To help you with your research I've compiled a list of tips to support you:

Health Insurance Research Tips

1. Relevance: Ensure all areas of cover are relevant to you (e.g., full comprehensive insurance covering children and pregnancy is unlikely to be important to you if you are a single man),

2. Flexibility: Look for products where you can pick and choose sections to suit your needs as such products are often very good value for money.

3. Limited Cover Plans: These are often cheap and worth considering in particular scenarios such as if

you are over 55 years of age or vulnerable to cancer. However, these can be restrictive as they only cover major illnesses.

4. Specialist Plans: These cover specific needs; for example, convalescence care plans for older people, professional care and support with shopping, cleaning and cooking to full nursing care which can be important to avoid prolonged hospital stays hence other risks associated with hospital stays.

5. Increase Your Excess: This is similar to car insurance, where the higher the excess, the more you can reduce your premium.

6. Choose a Waiting Period: Agreeing to a reasonable waiting period can reduce your premium; for example, if the NHS cannot provide treatment locally within six weeks your policy can arrange an alternative.

7. No Claims Discounts: Similar to car insurance, there's a range of offers available here, for example some may offer 10% a year working up to 50% for eight years if you don't make a claim on the policy, others may offer reduced premiums so long as the claims you make are small and less than a certain figure.

8. Hospital Choice: Some insurers reduce their premiums by restricting you to selected hospitals, whereas with other insurers you can pick and choose, even considering hospitals abroad. Consider doing a background check on the choice of hospitals you have.

9. Buy Online: As with most things nowadays, buying insurance online can give you access to discounts of up to 10%.

10. Avoid using comparison websites and always talk to an advisor for informed advice.

11. Keep Healthy: The nature of health insurance is such that if you stay healthy and ensure you are less of a health risk your insurance stays down, and many insurers offer incentives to this effect, while others charge higher prices to smokers and the obese.

Alternatives ways to invest in your health include:

- Critical Illness Cover: This often involves insurance against a range of serious health conditions such as cancer or a stroke. It tends to involve a lump sum pay out if you are diagnosed with such a condition, which you can use as you see fit.

- Health Care Cash Plans: There are a wide range of plans available, with some starting from as little as £1.00 per week.[4] This enables you to claim back the cost of certain basic health services or treatments such as dental work, physiotherapy and optical cover after paying for them upfront. There is usually an annual limit on how much you can claim.

- High Interest Account: I've included this as it is useful where you have loved ones who may not be entitled to receive health services from the NHS such as family abroad or even yourself as you get to keep the interest generated. In such cases you may find it useful to open an account and commit to saving a small amount every month, which could then be accessed in the event of 'health events.' This is especially prevalent in Singapore, where it is referred to as 'Medisave,' a state-run compulsory medical savings account for the working population.[14] Such accounts can be very effective in mobilizing private financial resources.[14]

When to Make That Step?

As far as health insurance goes, there is no time like the present!

The younger and healthier you are the easier and cheaper it will be for you to get health insurance, unlike car insurance, which tends to reduce with age, health insurance is quite the opposite as for most people the chances of being diagnosed with a major illness increases with age, similarly from an insurance point of view you become more of a risk.

To conclude, it is vital to invest effort, time and money in your health. From a financial standpoint, whatever road you decide to go down be sure to do your research and ask questions. This is important as rarely does one size fit all. In some cases, you may find you're better off going down the savings route, in others insurance may be an option, there isn't a right or wrong answer.

Fact is, if we all invest in our health then we would all be making a contribution towards reducing strains on the NHS and ensuring it stays true to its founding principles.

REFERENCES:

1. The Kings Fund, 2014. Commission on Future of Health and Social Care in England. The UK Private Health Market.
2. www.bupa.co.uk/health/health-insurance/health-insurance-guide. Accessed December 2016.
3. Obamacarefacts.com. Accessed November 2016.
4. Association of Medical Insurers and Intermediaries (AMII). http://amii.org.uk/faq. Accessed December 2016.
5. Mossialos E, Dixon A, Figuero J Et al. European Observatory on Health care Systems Series. Funding Health care: Options For Europe, 2002.
6. Savigny D and Adam T. Alliance for Health Policy and Health Systems, World Health Organisation (WHO), 2009. Systems Thinking for Health Systems Strengthening.
7. Cylus J, Richardson E, Findley L et al. European Observatory on Health Systems and Policies, World Health Organisation (WHO), 2015. Health Systems in Transition: United Kingdom Health System Review. 17(5): 25- 138.
8. http://www.nhs.uk/NHSEngland/thenhs/nhshistory/Pages/NHShistory1948.aspx.
9. http://www.nhs.uk/NHSEngland/thenhs/about/Pages/overview.aspx.
10. Pension and Insurance Working Group. Department of Health, January, 2014. Developing Products for Social Care.
11. Kate Barker (Chairman). Kings Fund, 2014. Final Report of the Independent Commission on the Future of Health and Social Care in England- A New Settlement for Health and Social Care.
12. Allyson Pollock. Medico-legal Journal, May 2008 (Medico-legal Society Meeting). Public Health Meets Law: Are there Sufficient Legal Safeguards to Ensure Access to Public Health

Care for All? Med Leg J, 2008; 72(4): 118- 132.

13. Pollock A and Roderick P. Medico-legal Journal, Nov 2015. Duty to Care and Universal Access to Health: In Defense of a Duty to Care and Provide Universal Access to Health in The Face of Limited Resources. Med Legal J, 2015; 83(4): 172- 184.

14. Lim MK. Annals of the Academy of Medicine Singapore, Aug 2005. Transforming Singapore Health Care: Public- Private Partnership. Ann Acad Med Singapore, 2005; 34(7): 461-7.

15. Keck CW and Reed G. American Journal of Public Health, Aug 2012. The Curious Case of Cuba. Am J Public Health, 2012; 102(8): e13- e22. Doi: 10.2015/AJPH.2012.300822

16. WHO Country Statistics for Cuba, France, the United Kingdom and the United States of America. http://www.who.int/countries. Accessed December 2016.

13

GAME CHANGING
HEALTH PRINCIPLES

"Every human being is the author
of his own health or disease."
— Prince Gautama Siddhartha,
Buddhism's founder, 563-483 B.C

This final chapter of the book is about you. Unlike many other things in life, health gives you the freedom to write your own story. This is because you determine the returns by deciding the 'how' as well as the 'what' you put into it.

Now, if you're one of the many people that has ever struggled with a health issue or indeed are currently struggling with a particular health issue then I would like to encourage you to change your game plan. You see, winning in personal health is a bit like sports – the difference between winning and losing is the game plan, and a team or individual's ability and willingness to adapt when things aren't working as planned. More importantly, everyone on the team and the peripheries must be in sync. Similarly, your health comprises of different elements, which must all be worked on in sync, working on just one aspect, for example your diet, is not enough to be healthy. Likewise, you should be willing to make changes when you fail to achieve desired results.

There is an old African proverb that says that 'the journey of a thousand miles starts with one step'; similarly, changing any aspect of your health starts with *just* one step. Living healthy is an ongoing process so any change you make has to be for the 'long haul' and this is where having principles will help.

As I draw the curtain on this book, I would like to leave you with some *'Game Changing Principles'*. I genuinely believe these will help you achieve and sustain a healthy lifestyle.

PRINCIPLE 1

Take a Step-by-Step Approach

If there is one thing in life that is constant, it is 'change.' The question is what kind of change are you working towards? Are you looking at regressive or progressive change?

More often than not, doing nothing about your health will ultimately result in regressive change. This in essence means an increased vulnerability to various illnesses or conditions. On the flip side, choosing to do the right thing will result in progressive change with respect to your health. I've used the words regressive and progressive because health improvement is a continuous process.

It is not about making radical changes to your diet for instance, rather it is about making sustainable changes.

These are easier to make when effected gradually and progressively. For instance you may decide to reduce your intake of fizzy drinks this week and then reduce further the following week until stopping altogether. Alternatively you may start by doing 1 hour's exercise per week and gradually build up to the recommended 150 minutes exercise per week by adding 15 minutes extra each week.

So, keep it simple by relaxing and committing to little changes on a regular basis. Ultimately this will lead to big and sustainable improvements in your health.

PRINCIPLE 2

Focus on Habits Rather than Effort

Have you ever heard the saying we are creatures of habit? Well, when it comes to health behaviours and actions this statement couldn't be truer. For most of us, our entire lifestyle is based on habits we have formed over several years largely influenced by our upbringing, culture and environments. Consequently, to think that health-related habits can be changed overnight and subsequently maintained is somewhat naïve and setting yourself up for disappointment. You see, *living a healthy lifestyle is not about maximal and unsustainable efforts; rather, it is about habitual developments.*

The lack of realization of this simple fact is the reason many end up frustrated in their efforts to improve their health. For example, many people lose weight only to regain it as they gradually slip back into old eating habits. Thus, rather than focus on changing such habits in the long term, their short-term focus on efforts to reduce their weight means that they struggle to keep the weight off as they are unable to sustain the drastic efforts they've made in the short term to lose weight. Habitual developments take time, so the key message here is to note your bad habits and their origins and decipher steps to overcome such habits within a realistic timeframe.

PRINCIPLE 3

Set Short- and Long-Term Goals

It is important to set both short and long-term goals. However, you may find that your short-term goals can be set up as a series of steps towards long-term goals. For example, it might be that you aim to lose half a kilogram each week with the ultimate aim of dropping a dress size (which according to anecdotal evidence equates to a loss of five to eight kilograms for most) within six months. This may vary between individuals, but six months would be a reasonable timeframe for most people to achieve this long-term goal.

As you set your goals, visualize the end results you would like to see and make a plan towards achieving the goal. This should be from an all-round viewpoint; for example, rather than focus on starving yourself to death in a bid to be stick thin, title your goal 'achieving a healthy weight' then note down various actions and short-term goals required to do this, which should entail a better diet with the right balance of nutrients and increased levels of physical activity. The beauty of this is that you will automatically find that you don't just lose weight; rather, you will lose it in a healthy and sustainable manner as a result of improved eating and exercise habits.

PRINCIPLE 4

Create a Reward System

Many people find it hard to go the distance when it comes to achieving their health goals. A good example is the number of people who resolve to increase their fitness at the beginning of the year but find that they're struggling by year end or even before.

You may find that rewarding yourself for achieving short- and long-term goals will help motivate you to go the distance. Creating a reward system will help you get through the tough times and over various health barriers. Rewards are strong motivational incentives and are what the whole concept of sports is based on. Think about an athlete or sports team. A whole season is dedicated to putting in 100% commitment and effort in the hope that they are able to get a prize and reward at the end of the season. The individuals in the team may go through hell individually and collectively, but by keeping their eye on the prize they stay committed to the goal. Give yourself an incentive to stay committed when you are tempted to deviate from your plan or goal.

PRINCIPLE 5

Live Active

This doesn't necessarily mean daily visits to the gym or running a marathon, rather it is about *making being active an actual lifestyle.* For example, it could entail walking to a colleague in the office rather than sending an email or parking further away from where you're going so you are forced to walk. It could even entail standing on the train or bus rather than sitting. Many people struggle to achieve the recommended 150 minutes per week recommended by Public Health England, but if you make 'being active a lifestyle' you'll find it is easier to meet that target as you can clock minutes from various activities you're doing as part of your regular day-to-day living. For example, let's say you trek three times a week briskly to the train station for 20 minutes each time, right there you can knock 60 minutes off the 150 minutes. Do you get the picture now? Remember, in this case every little bit counts!

PRINCIPLE 6

Be Creative

The key point here is *'to do you'* as, contrary to popular belief, there isn't an exact formula or science in the method you take to be healthy, *the successful formula or approach is one that works for you.* In other words, don't be hard on yourself because you're current approach that worked for someone else isn't working for you. Rather, think about what would work for you as a person or how to adapt a strategy that worked for someone else for you. In other words, create your own unique healthy lifestyle with what you have learnt, the 'how' is solely up to you.

PRINCIPLE 7

Make and Maintain Positive Connections

This is vital as no man is an island and we all need positive relationships for our health and wellbeing. Depending on where such occurs, you may find that through positive associations (in an exercise setting) you are also able to improve your mental, physical and social health and wellbeing simultaneously. In addition, remember 'iron sharpens iron', so making positive connections can also serve as a form of encouragement to help you stay the course to achieve your health-related goals.

PRINCIPLE 8

Let Hygiene be your #1 Barrier to Infections

Hygiene is seldom mentioned when many people talk about health. Even when it is mentioned it is rarely in its entirety. Hygiene as a preventative measure is right up there if not at the top of the list with other preventative interventions. As you look to improve your health don't forget to practise good hygiene whether it concerns you as a person, your sexual habits, the food you eat or your wider environment.

PRINCIPLE 9

Win Through Growth

Phil Jackson, arguably the NBA's most successful coach, explained his secret to winning championships continuously was through ensuring his team were committed to learning and growing daily. Similarly, improving your health means a commitment to growing and applying new and relevant knowledge, often gained by engaging with experts rather than relying on the media.

The journey starts with you wanting to win, and then you've got to commit to growing and evolving through any setbacks you may encounter along the way. Most of us encounter different health challenges at any given time. Try not to be hard on yourself or throw in the towel when struggling with a particular aspect of your health. Rather, consider learning from failed attempts and be willing to try a new approach. Don't be afraid to talk as you may find that talking to someone gives you a better perspective on things.

PRINCIPLE 10

Take a Moderate Approach

Moderation and balance is key to improving your overall health and wellbeing. In this book I have tried to cover a wide range of topics that all feed into your health, whether it be through supplementation or your belief or the need to invest in your health. This is aside from the key elements of physical, social and mental wellbeing. All of the topics addressed are interlinked, but whatever plans you create or goals you set with regards improving your health, please do not become obsessed with numbers or your desire to be healthier. Be moderate and take a balanced approach to improving your health. Remember *slow and steady often wins the race.*

I hope that you have found this book useful and are able to use what I call *'game changing health principles'* to apply what you have learnt.

An important reality of our time is that many health systems are struggling to deliver on health. This is in part because health needs outstrip capacity in most countries. The onus is therefore on you to rely a little less on government, fate, or faith (which must be actioned to become a reality anyhow).

Remember, *'today's choices will impact your health and productivity today and tomorrow.'* Therefore be sure to choose and invest wisely today.

Before closing the book, why don't you take a few minutes to develop and write your own health improvement plan; alternatively, check out HIP (health improvement programme) on the website www. truthabouthealthexposed.com, which provides practical support and guidance to help you live healthier.

.